PIRTON - A VILLAGE IN ANGUISH

The Story of the 30 Men from a Hertfordshire Village who died in WW1

by Derek Jarrett

Published by Pirton Local History Group

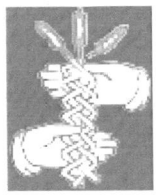

Published 2009

ISBN 978-0-9512103-3-8

Printed by The Lavenham Press Ltd.

****

All rights reserved. No part of this publication may be produced, stored in a retrieval system, or transmitted in any form, or by any means, electronic, mechanical, photocopying, recording or otherwise, without the prior permission of the author.

This book is inspired by and dedicated to the men of Pirton who fought in the 1914-1918 War.

The author is indebted to the many Pirton villagers, relatives of the men who died and others who have helped him in writing the stories of the 30 Pirton men whose ordinary lives were suddenly changed – and ended – by the Great War, 1914-1918.

Particular thanks are due to the late Lynda Smith whose research into the names of men on War Memorials provided a starting point and to Clare Baines whose extraordinary knowledge of local families was a constant help. A full list of acknowledgements is given at the end of the book.

However careful the research, errors are inevitable and these should be attributed to the author. He will be interested to hear from anyone who can add to any part of the book and can be contacted on Jarretts@idnet.com

---

Further copies can be obtained from the author Jarretts@idnet.com
or from local bookshops & Pirton Village Stores

CONTENTS

A Village in Anguish — 1

Company Sergeant Major Frank Cannon — 4
    First name on the Memorial: a professional footballer

Private Frank Abbiss — 7
    Emigrant to Canada returns to die for his country

Private Frank Handscombe — 10
    First of the Pirton men killed in the Battle of the Somme

Private Joseph French — 13
    A farm labourer: the second Pirton Somme death

Private John Parsell — 16
    With Pirton mates as a shell kills him

Private Alfred Raymond Jenkins — 19
    Pirton's 'Big fellow': another victim of the Somme

Private Arthur Walker — 22
    Leaves a wife and child after dying from wounds

Private Sidney Baines — 25
    Family's added grief at never knowing his burial place

Private Edward Charles Burton — 28
    Killed four days short of his 20th birthday

Private Harry Crawley — 31
    1917: another year – another death

Private George Trussell — 34
    The gulf between war leaders and the soldiers

Private Joseph Handscombe — 37
    Village family lose second son

Corporal Harry Smith — 40
    Killed on the first day of Passchendaele

Private William Baines — 43
    Second Pirton death at the horror of Passchendaele

Lance Corporal William Thomas Hill — 46
    Love for a Pirton lass brought him to the village

Corporal Albert Titmuss — 49
'Thou leavest me to grieve' – his widow mourns for 53 years

Sergeant Fred Burton — 52
Cambridge servant, Berkshire butler and soldier

Private Walter Reynolds — 55
Of six soldier sons, one gassed and now one killed

Lance Corporal Arthur Odell — 58
Old village family suffers a terrible loss

Lance Sergeant Charles Wilshere — 61
One of the oldest Pirton soldiers killed

Private Bert Wilson — 64
Son of Martha, the 'village medicine lady'

Private Henry Chamberlain, DCM — 67
Pirton's tough guy, winner of a major bravery award

Private George Charlick — 70
London born, son of Pirton special constable

Private Frederick Anderson — 73
Declared unfit, he labours on and dies of pneumonia

Gunner Albert Reynolds — 76
A nature lover – even in time of war

Private Jack Pearce — 79
Phyllis tells the story of her two dead brothers

Private Fred Baines — 82
The sixth 'Pirton terrier' to be killed

Gunner Arthur Lake — 85
First of three Pirton men to die after the Armistice

Private Frank Abbiss — 88
Died in Egypt on Christmas Day 1918

Private Frederick Odell — 91
Died of terrible injuries five months after War ends

The Aftermath — 94

Acknowledgements — 96

A VILLAGE IN ANGUISH

When Mr Benjamin Crowther, 'The Master' at the village school looked at the children under his charge in late 1898, he could not have imagined that sixteen of those present would be dead within 20 years; killed in the First World War. By the end of the *'War to end all Wars'*, there were 30 names ready to be written on the Pirton War Memorial; of these 26 attended Pirton School.

As his pupils came under the stern gaze of Mr Crowther, he saw that many were ill-clothed. The village population, apart from a few wealthy landowners and some who had a trade, consisted of poorly paid farm labourers and their strawplaiting wives and children. Some pupils were from single parent families; most families continued to live in the village of their birth. Life for the villagers, mostly with large families, was poor and hard, but it was peaceful and largely predictable. In a few years all this changed.

By 1914 Europe was sliding inescapably into a conflict which few wanted, but which grew daily more certain. The building blocks for a war were well in place; colonial and economic rivalry, a furious arms race, an Archduke's assassination, tortuous alliances and total distrust all stoked a smouldering Europe. The German invasion of neutral Belgium sealed Europe's fate; not only the immediate cause of Britain declaring war on 4th August 1914, but a great rallying cry to the British. The nation was filled with a passionate sense of righteousness and increasing patriotism. No longer a smouldering Europe, but one of uncontrollable flames.

From the death of the first Pirton War Memorial name in February 1916, war deaths from the village averaged one a month. Five of the thirty men were under twenty-one years old, fifteen were in their 20s, eight in their 30s and two had passed their fortieth birthday. Most were single, but eight were married and of these, five had children. Twenty three of the 30 men died as privates, the others ranged from a lance corporal to the highest ranking, a company sergeant major. This was not a village of officers. To add to the grief, in each of four families two brothers were killed.

This generation of war-dead had been the first to receive the benefits of free education provided through the village school that had opened in 1877. This helped some leave the ranks of simple agricultural workers, a change accelerated as farming became more mechanised and needing less workers. Some had moved away before the outbreak of war; one to Canada, others to London and its suburbs to work in the building trade.

Their parents generally remained within the village; few people moved in. There was little attraction to do so, for employment was unlikely and the day when affluent people would move into a picturesque village was decades away. This relative poverty of Pirton is reflected in the downward spiral of population after 1880.

It appears that twenty of the men on the War Memorial still lived in the parish in 1914, suggesting that more than 1 in 10 of war-age

From the children at the village school at the beginning of the 20th century, many were to serve in the Great War; some to die.

village men was killed. Of the others, it is known that four lived in nearby towns, five in London or the Home Counties and Albert Abbiss in Canada.

The war years were a time of almost unbearable anguish, as villagers waited for news of their loved ones; there would have been few Pirton households untouched by war-death grief.

Various economic forces had shaped the lives of these men, of which poverty, often aggravated by the size of the family, was the strongest. In addition to the influence of parents and an intricate network of family links, the School, St. Mary's Church, the Methodist Chapel and the employing farms were influential. Increasingly, the nearby town of Hitchin became important and London, especially as a source of employment, was fast becoming significant.

Many of the young men were in the prime of life, thickset, rubicund and of considerable strength.

By contrast, their elders were stooped, with gnarled hands, often riddled with rheumatism as the result of a life spent outdoors in all weathers.

The soldiers from the village were but a few among the thousands who were *'the lions led by donkeys'*. The real causes of the war were ill-understood by politicians and army generals, certainly not by the Pirton men. The many who volunteered for King and Country did so through loyalty, some for adventure. Sheer emotion and human guts were the driving forces of these brave men. Some of the young men from the village were in the first contingent of the Herts Regiment to go to France in August 1914. From 1916 onwards, a few may have been conscripted as the numbers volunteering fell short of battle needs, fuelled by the terrible casualty rate.

Whilst most on the Village War Memorial shared having been born in Pirton, going to the same

School, playing and growing up together in an innocent childhood, each name on the Memorial tells a story of individual grief. They were called upon to do something totally alien to them – moving from a peaceful landscape to hell, from farming to war.

Four of the men whose names were inscribed on the War Memorial were neither born in Pirton nor attended the village school. Their places on the Memorial were gained through other village links; one marrying a village girl, one working on a Pirton farm, another by his parents moving to the village and a fourth by moving into the parish before a boundary change. There are names that may have been missed off the Memorial, but that is another story; perhaps to be corrected in the future.

A wonderful aspect of researching the stories of the Pirton men is the contribution of so many people. Present and former villagers, some related to the 30 men, provided rich information. Grace Maidment remembers the gun-carriage bearing Fred Odell's body coming into the village in 1919 and Phyllis Pearce talked of her family in which two of her brothers were killed, but whom she was too young to remember. Then, there was Audrey Ford who had lovingly kept the card bearing the news of her uncle's death.

Whilst pictures of sixteen of the men have been located, some are from the poor quality wartime newspapers, reflecting the austerity of the times.

Most of the men died in the central battle areas of northern France and Flanders and some of their resting places bear names that are terribly familiar – the Somme, Arras and Cambrai.

People may have learnt few lessons from the Great War, but the 30 names deserve to live on for ever as an important part of Pirton's history.

The village school still proudly displays its wonderful tribute to the men who attended their school and went on to serve King and Country in the Great War.

From the 30 names on the Village War Memorial, 26 attended the school.

Soldier 1: Died Tuesday 15th February 1916

COMPANY SERGEANT MAJOR FRANK CANNON
FIRST NAME ON THE MEMORIAL: A PROFESSIONAL FOOTBALLER

Eighteen months into the Great War; Gallipoli had fallen, the Somme carnage not yet begun. The streets in Pirton were bereft of young men, except for the occasional khaki figure on leave from the inferno in north-western Europe.

By February 1916 more than 200 men who had been born in Pirton were fighting for King and Country, some volunteering even before the war had started. From those first eighteen months of the war not a single name was to be inscribed on the Village War Memorial; not a single Pirton fatality. The North Hertfordshire newspapers were full of war deaths; Pirton seemed alone of the local villages without one. However, a harbinger of Pirton village deaths came in September 1915, when Private Herbert John Clarke, father of ten young children, from nearby Offley was killed in France. He was well known in Pirton and related to several serving village soldiers. Then, in the middle of that nineteenth month of the war the first Pirton death was announced which would later be recorded on the Village War Memorial.

Frank Cannon was born in Hitchin, some four miles from Pirton. He was the third son of the ten children of Martha and John Cannon, a fruiterer working out of Churchyard, next to St. Mary's Church in Hitchin, where the family lived. Frank was born on 8th November 1885 and attended the school in the shadow of the fourteenth century church.

Leaving school, Frank worked in a Hitchin solicitors' office. However, by the age of fifteen, he was making his mark as a footballer with the town team. After playing with them for seven seasons, he joined Queens Park Rangers as a professional, though still continuing at the solicitors' office. He represented Hertfordshire on many occasions between 1902 - 1908 and won

A fine centre-forward with two major London clubs

several gold medals with Hitchin. He was described as '*A dashing player and good dribbler with a fine shot*'. One of his finest goals was in the 1907-08 FA Charity Shield Final when Queens Park Rangers, the Southern League Champions, drew 1-1 with Manchester United, the Football League Champions. He later scored a hat-trick against West Ham in the Southern League and instantly captured the opposition's interest. In 1909, he moved to West Ham and in his three first team matches was never on the losing side; scoring in their 5-0 victory over Norwich at Upton Park in 1910.

Frank, a keen all-round sportsman, was also an excellent diver and a member of the Blue Cross Swimming Club in Hitchin.

But Frank's interest was not only in sport, for in August 1909 he married Violet Maud Clark, originally from Cheshunt where her father had a general store. For a time, the newly married couple lived in Hitchin where their first child, Margaret, was born in the late summer of 1910. Less than six months later they moved to Gillingham in Kent as boarders of a retired naval pensioner. Frank, still a professional footballer, was busy learning skills as a nurseryman; perhaps he had an eye on the days when he would have to retire from football. However, it was not long before he returned to his native North Hertfordshire where he started a smallholding on West Mill Farm. The family moved into one of the cottages near the large farmhouse, the home of Ernest Bowman the local flour miller. At that time, West Mill, which lies by the River Oughton, was within the parish of Pirton; the reason why a Hitchin man came to be on the Pirton Memorial. (He is on the Hitchin War Memorial, too).

With the outbreak of war in 1914, Lord Kitchener appealed for recruits. Frank quickly responded, enlisting in Hitchin by the second week of September 1914 in the 11th Battalion the Essex Regiment, bearing the regimental number 14982. He did not go abroad immediately and managed a few games with Fulham in the early months of the war. He was later in a training camp at Shoreham and it was from there, in August 1915, that he was posted to the Western Front.

In Pirton, like every other village and town in the country, war fever ran high, not least with the Vicar writing in February 1915, after a village event to raise recruits:

'All patriotic members of the audience must feel ashamed...when after all the trouble taken by friends, including our MP, to come over, not one single recruit was secured, while other Pirton men are risking their lives for us!'

But Frank escaped such godly wroth when, in the October parish magazine, his name appeared as one of the twenty-three men under the heading, *'Pirton Patriotism'*. It seems that he and one of his brothers, Robert, had enlisted on the same day for they had consecutive regimental numbers. A third brother, Ralph, also joined up.

Certainly this strong ex-centre forward, by this time a father of three young children, was in France with the 11th Battalion on 31st August 1915 as the war began to get more and more bogged down in rarely shifting trench lines. Thirty year-old Frank made rapid progress through the ranks; he must have shown real leadership qualities. He became the highest ranking soldier on the Village WW1 Memorial. Pirton was not a place of officers.

A short period of leave enabled him to get back to see his family at the beginning of 1916, but by the end of January, Acting Company Sergeant Major Cannon was near Ypres, a small Flemish market town close to the French border. He was in one of the many foul and stinking trenches, even though cigarette butts and matches had to be removed for an officer's inspection. He was in that trench for sixteen consecutive days until his death on 15th February. That fatal Tuesday was to have been his last day before a break from the front-line fighting, when a shell fell nearby and he was hit by shrapnel in the back. He died a short while later.

First to receive the news was younger brother Ralph who was in a nearby forward position. The news was also quickly sent back to England by Sergeant Martin, a member of Frank's regiment who came from Hitchin.

He was buried in the Potijze Burial Ground Cemetery Ypres (Ieper), West-Vlaanderen in Belgium (Flanders) – (ref. H10). Potijze is a small hamlet, now really a suburb of Ypres. On the headstone marking his grave is a private inscription, *'Always remembered by those at home'*.

News of his death quickly reached Pirton and anguish must have affected every villager, for many knew of footballer Frank Cannon and all knew someone who was fighting. Whilst newspaper reports were full of casualties, this grim news must have touched each Pirton heart. Five days after his death, the Revd E.W.Langmore, Vicar of St. Mary's in the village, began his sermon by sympathising with the family, *'Who have been residing at West Mill for some time'*.

It is uncertain where his widow, Violet Maud, was living; maybe at 87 Walsworth Road in Hitchin. The youngest of their three children was only a few weeks old when Frank was killed. Certainly his widow was living in Walsworth Road in the 1920s.

In the August 1918 parish magazine, Frank Cannon was shown as one of the nineteen Pirton men who had died; others names were added later. One of the most generous donations, ten shillings, to the intended War Memorial was from 'Mrs Cannon'. In addition to the Pirton and Hitchin War Memorials, he is also remembered at the Essex Regiment private Chapel in Warley, Brentwood which was occupied by the regiment for over 100 years.

The first eighteen months of the war had not seen a Pirton man die, but following Frank Cannon's death, a further 29 deaths were to be inscribed on the Village War Memorial.

The Essex Regiment Chapel is located in Warley, Brentwood, where CSM Frank Cannon and all other men of the Regiment are remembered.

 *Soldier 2: Died Wednesday 29th March 1916*

PRIVATE ALBERT ABBISS

EMIGRANT TO CANADA RETURNS TO DIE FOR HIS COUNTRY

When Albert Abbiss left England and crossed the magnificent, unpopulated plains and mountains of Canada to settle in British Columbia, he cannot have imagined returning a few years later to the battle horrors of Belgium.

In spite of living in Canada for seven years, Albert was every inch a Pirton man. The Abbiss family was a large one, stretching to many households in the village. He was born on 16th November 1887, the eldest son of Frank and Elizabeth Abbiss. Not long after his birth, the family moved briefly to the neighbouring village of Holwell, but returned to Pirton, joining the several Abbiss families in the dilapidated, thatched cottages on Great Green.

He attended Pirton School and whilst leaving at the normal age of thirteen he was of the first generation of village families to receive a formal education. He first became a local ploughboy, but his schooling and ambition caused him, a few years later, to take a giant step. Farming, was employing fewer local lads and many young men were moving from the village to gain work in other places. Finsbury Park was becoming a popular destination for some to work on the building work relating to the railways, but Albert decided to try his luck abroad. His family must have been anxious when 20 year-old Albert left for Canada. Amid a mixture of good wishes and tears he set out on Thursday 20th June 1907 together with two other village lads, Tobias Cherry and Arthur Baines. They left Euston on the midnight train for Liverpool, leaving on the S.S.Virginian built for the Allan Line two years previously, and landing in Quebec on 29th June. The ship and the great expanses of Canada must have been hugely exciting to him. He crossed the Rockies and arrived in New Westminster, once the capital of British Columbia and only a short distance from the rapidly growing Vancouver.

Life was tough, but Albert was an industrious young man and after working on the land for a while, took several other jobs and seems to have prospered. During his time in British Columbia, other friends from Pirton joined him in 1909; his brother Tom three years later. Albert closely followed news of the rising European conflict. He became a member of the 'Active Militia', able-bodied men locally recruited to defend against invasion or rebellion, in support of British

1907: Set out for Canada from Liverpool on the SS Virginian.

7

Description of Albert Abbiss on Enlistment.

Apparent Age 27 years 4 months.
Height: 5 ft 8 ins.
Girth when fully expanded: 40 ins.
Range of expansion: 3½ ins.
Complexion: Medium
Eyes: Grey
Hair: Brown

Distinctive marks: Three vaccination marks on left arm. Letters "T.H.C. over heart, cross and anchor" tattooed on right fore arm.

Regular Forces. For Albert this was a fore-runner of becoming a full-scale soldier and he joined the 7th Battalion Canadian Infantry (British Columbia Regiment), which had been formed in the summer of 1914.

From his attestation papers, the document which he signed as his oath of allegiance on 13th March 1915, we can picture a little of this young soldier. He was 5ft 8ins tall, had three vaccination marks on his left arm and tattooed on his right forearm were the letters THC over a cross and anchor. The source of these three letters will probably never be known.

It seems that between 1907 and 1915 Albert returned three times to England, indicating his love of family, friends and homeland and a growing income. It is well recorded that he was 'kind-hearted and a good son'. The third journey, as a Private A. Abbiss, 429001, of the 7th Battalion Canadian Infantry and thus of the Canadian Overseas Expeditionary Force, was his last.

This 28 year-old Canadian private arrived in England in June 1915 for training somewhere in the country, managing to visit his family in Pirton once more. Two months later this stocky, fit man used to much travelling, left for France. He wrote home regularly, his final letter reaching his parents a week before his death in March 1916.

The war that Albert joined had become increasing confused and it is not often possible to know exactly where men fought. It is likely that he was in one of the many actions around St. Elois on the road running south from Ypres towards Messines. There was a salient (a 'finger' of land projecting into territory held by the enemy) on slightly higher ground - including an artificial earth bank called "The Mound" – held by the Germans. It gave them an excellent position over British trenches and roads. This had been the scene of almost continuous mine warfare during 1915, with both sides actively engaged. On Monday 27th March, six British mines were fired totalling 73,000lbs of charges, but even so the Germans retained their positions. Craters devastated the last remnants of the countryside. Not long afterwards an artillery corporal was completely overawed by the size of the craters, *'I saw the effect of the mines. The size of the crater really petrified me. I mean, it was as big as a cathedral'*.

Whilst uncertain as to the exact place of Albert's death, it is known that he was killed by a shell burst on Wednesday 29th March 1916, a year and two weeks after signing up. He was buried in the Berks. Cemetery Extension, Comines-Warneton in Hainaut, Belgium (Burial ref. 3.B.20). 149 Canadians are buried there.

In a letter to Albert's parents, arriving in Pirton on 4th April, the serving chaplain Rev Louis W Moffitt, wrote:

> *'He was killed by a shell which burst quite close to him on the road beside their billet, where they were in reserve. It will be a little comfort to you to know that he was instantly killed and did not suffer. We buried him that evening at the battalion cemetery on the slope of Hill 63, near Plug-street Wood in the presence of his comrades. Before we left there, a cross was erected.'*

Pte Purser, also of the Canadian Regiment, who was described as a *'close chum'* of Albert's sister Rose, wrote,

> *'I know it will be a hard blow to your mother so I write to you. All I can say to comfort you is that Alfred** met a painless end. I have a few of his things which I will send to you at the first opportunity, as I know they were obtained for that purpose. Alfred was respected by all who knew him and I for one will miss the best friend I ever had.'*

The First World War claimed the lives of over 60,000 Canadians, over one-tenth of the men who crossed the Atlantic to go to war. The Canadian 'Book of Remembrance – First World War' records all the names. Alphabetically Albert appears third in this Book of Remembrance; chronologically he appears second on Pirton's War Memorial. The fourth name in the Canadian Remembrance Book is Arthur David Abbiss of the Manitoba regiment who died seven months after Albert. Arthur's parents lived in Hitchin and he was probably a distant cousin of Albert. Their lives and deaths followed similar routes; both born in North Hertfordshire, both emigrating to Canada and both killed in 1916.

Albert's parents are buried in St. Mary's churchyard in Pirton. His brother Tom, who also joined a Canadian Regiment in June 1915, survived the war. Ninety years on, the craters close to where Albert Abbiss died are now ponds, used for private fishing and swimming.

**In reporting Albert's death, two local newspapers referred to him as Alfred. It is sincerely hoped that this was a careless error by the newspapers, not by those who wrote letters of sympathy to his parents.

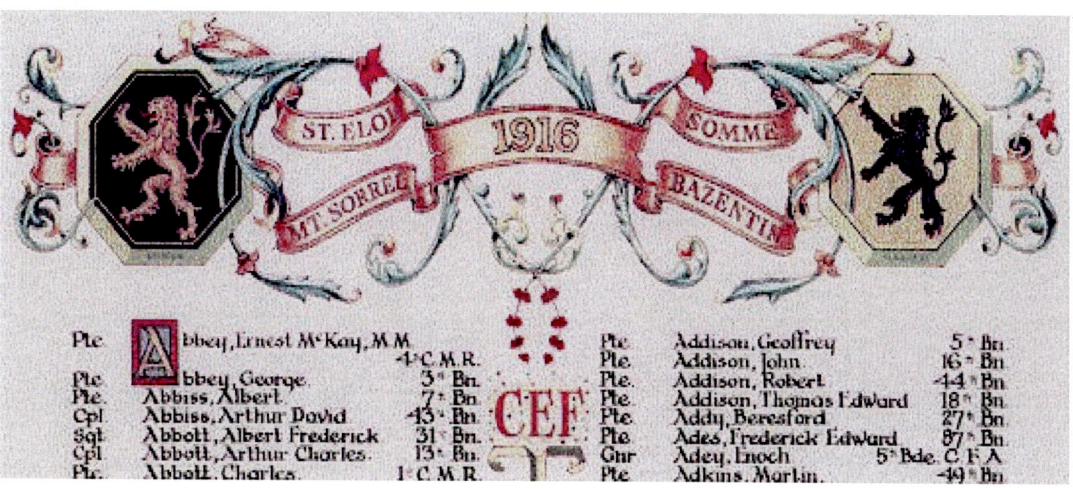

The Canadian 'Book of Remembrance' records the 60,000 men who died in the war. The third name recorded is Private Albert Abbiss.

Soldier 3: Died Tuesday 11th July 1916

PRIVATE FRANK HANDSCOMBE

THE FIRST PIRTON MAN KILLED IN THE BATTLE OF THE SOMME

Saturday 1st July remains a terrible and tragic day in British history, for it saw the start of the Battle of the Somme, one of the most senseless actions in a war renowned for its senselessness. Historians may argue about the battle, but the image of the Somme is one of unbroken and monumental horror, the reality of trench warfare.

That first day of July 1916 was a calamity of a kind previously unknown. British casualties on that single day were 57,000, of whom 19,240 were killed.

It was the biggest British army ever sent in to battle; 27 divisions on a fifteen mile front. The men had arrived, burdened with much equipment, but singing their music-hall songs to accompany their marching. Each carried tools for trenching,

over 200 rounds of ammunition, gas mask, wire-cutters, Mills bomb, and groundsheet – around seventy pounds of equipment each.

Amongst these thousands were young men who had been born, grown up and lived in the quietness of Pirton as well as in thousands of other hamlets, villages and towns. Men later spoke of an extraordinary camaraderie that existed in the trenches; that nothing like it could ever exist in civilian life. With some Pirton men, this camaraderie had deep roots; same school, same training camps and same battalion in which they found the same horrors of war.

The ensuing 140 days saw the deaths of over 400,000 British men, a similar number of Germans and over 200,000 French. The Somme culled a million men, a bloodbath of a monstrous kind. Amongst those soldiers were six Pirton men; Private Frank Handscombe was the first. His brother, killed nine months later near Arras, made them the first of four pairs of Pirton brothers to die.

The name of Handscombe goes back at least four centuries in Pirton and the family links continue to this day. In 1883 George Handscombe, a 41 old farm labourer, married Martha Dawson, aged 25; both of Pirton. Frank, born in 1894, was the eighth of ten children.

He attended the village school and, whilst great changes have taken place in the village in the intervening century, he would have passed and explored many of the same sights that the school children still enjoy today. When Frank was born, there were just over 200 houses in the village (now close to 500), but with a similar population as today. Most houses, better called cottages, were crowded with large families, with few of the cottages having more than four small rooms and the privy in the garden.

The Wesleyan Chapel that was so close to Frank Handscombe's heart. It was here that he led the Sunday School classes, frequently mentioned in his letters from the Front.

Frank, his parents and many siblings lived in a thatched cottage set back from the rough road, near to the present no. 17 Shillington Road. One of his older sisters, Jane, was the mother of Joe Titmuss and Margaret Ingram, and Margaret well remembers visiting her grandmother (Frank's mother) in the cottage later demolished (as was its successor).

The Handscombes were much involved with the village Methodist Chapel and to Frank his faith, reflected in his support of the Wesleyan Chapel, was a major force in his life. Even when he was at the Front, his letters indicated just how much God and his beloved chapel were in his thoughts and prayers. He was thirteen when the present chapel opened, but it was the older Wesleyan building lower down in High Street, then being used as a Sunday School, that was closest to Frank's heart. His was a fine, sensitive nature and his influence with the children in the Sunday school where he was teacher and secretary, was great and its continuing success was frequently mentioned in those war-time letters. His loss was much felt by the many children and adults whom he had known so well in the peaceful pre-war days at the Chapel. When Frank joined up, his Sunday school role was taken up by younger brother, Joseph.

After leaving school, Frank found local employment as a farm labourer. Sometime after 1911, he joined the growing number of Pirton men working around Finsbury Park in North London and it was from there, in 1915, that he enlisted at Mill Hill as Private 22173 in the 6th Bedfordshire Regiment. Only a month earlier he was reported as having given *'an encouraging report'* at the Pirton Wesleyan annual meeting. He went to France in the late spring of 1916.

At the beginning of July 1916, what became embalmed in the memory as the Battle of the Somme, started amid the already war-torn territory of a previously lovely countryside. The attack was preceded by an eight-day bombardment of the German lines. This was so intense that Field Marshall Haig expected to destroy the German forward defences enabling British troops to cross 'No Man's Land', taking the German front lines from the demoralised enemy. Twenty-seven divisions of men went into the attack, 750,000 men; the odds seemed heavily in this attacking force's favour. However, the bombardment had not destroyed either the German front line barbed wire nor the hastily, but heavily-built concrete bunkers. Added to which, many of the British artillery shells proved to be 'duds', quite ineffective. Advancing British troops were picked off like targets at a German fun fair. Haig's *'numbers game'* didn't work. The British artillery competed with the German machine-guns throughout that awful day.

Between the 1st and 21st of July, 30,038 British men died on that Western Front; Frank's regiment losing over 1400 men. As the fighting raged, there were 23 regimental deaths on 10th July. On the following, overcast day, Tuesday 11th, Frank was killed. He was 22; one of the first men to be buried at the Gordon Dump cemetery, Ovillers-La-Boissell, Somme (Ref V.J.5).

Frank's parents learnt some of the details of their son's death in a letter from Sergeant W Austin:

'I deeply regret to have to inform you of the sad death of your son Frank, who was killed on the morning of July 11th. He did not suffer any pain as death was instantaneous. I was his platoon sergeant, and thought it my duty to write to you. He was a good soldier and always did his duty. I was sorry to lose him as he was liked by all. I might mention that myself and two of my men buried him, and we put a cross over his grave with his name upon it.'

Pirton's Wesleyan Chapel was full on Sunday 30th July for a memorial service when some of Frank's words when joining the Bedfords the previous year were quoted: *'Perhaps, next year at this time I shall have made the great sacrifice'*.

Valerie Taylor, granddaughter of one of Frank's brothers, made an emotional trip to the cemetery in 2005.

'The site is down a farm track in open countryside, it was very quiet and peaceful and the cemetery was immaculately kept. It felt very strange to be probably the first in the family to visit there, but I was glad he was out in the fields similar to those he must have known as a boy and young man growing up in Pirton.'

Although not realised at the time, it was one of those awful acts of fate, that Frank's brother Joseph landed in France on the very day that Frank was killed. Joseph was killed just nine months later.

Frisby, another of his brothers, and his wife Kate named their own son, born in 1918, after Frank; in memory of this young soldier. Valerie Taylor can remember a 'medal' bearing the name Frank Handscombe, on a bedroom wall in her grandparents' house in Royal Oak Lane; it had been awarded to her Great Uncle Frank, the first Pirton death on the Somme in Picardy.

George, Frank's father, aged 77, died in 1919 and his mother, Martha, in 1931. Both are buried in Pirton St. Mary's churchyard.

The village memorial service for Private Frank Handscombe was held in the relatively new Methodist Chapel.

Soldier 4: Died Monday 4th September 1916

PRIVATE JOSEPH FRENCH

FARM LABOURER: THE SECOND PIRTON DEATH AT THE SOMME

Lying at the far end of the Chiltern Hills, Pirton is surrounded by open farm land; arable now, but with much mixed farming a hundred years ago. Until the 1880's, virtually all the young village men worked in the fields; the description *'agricultural labourer'* was the label recorded in census records. Girls went into service or worked as strawplaiters supplying the demands of Luton hat-making factories; boys into the fields. As agriculture became more mechanised, needing less workers, and children gained both in education and ambition from the village school, more young lads moved away for employment. Others remained in the village and Joseph French typified those who stayed to work in the local fields. A decade later he must have found the change from the quiet Pirton landscape to the war-torn land of the Somme, first exciting and then terrifying. Sadly, such men as Joseph were the unsung martyrs of this terrible war.

On 15th February 1879, William Henry French, aged 31, married Mary Ann Reynolds, aged 22, at St. Mary's; both had lived for many years in Pirton, although William had been born in Breachwood Green, a hamlet near Luton. At the time of their marriage, both worked in the most common occupations of the villagers; William a farm labourer, Mary a straw plaiter. Of at least ten children born to Mary, only three survived; health and wealth were not ingredients in this village with many families still showing late Victorian under-privilege with its features of poverty and poor nourishment.

Ten years after their marriage, Joseph was born on 14th April 1889. Sunday 4th August that year was a busy one at St. Mary's Church for there were five baptisms, all administered by the Rector of Higham Gobion; maybe Pirton's own Rev Loughborough was on holiday. Joseph remained their only son; Kate and Annie his sisters. He was always known as Joe, whose slight build could not disguise his toughness.

Leaving the village school, Joseph followed in the footsteps of his forebears, the land. He worked for Fred Coxall and later Thomas Franklin, who farmed out of Walnut Tree Farm. He continued to live with his parents, became an active member of the village football team and remained unmarried. One of Joseph's sisters, Annie, was the mother of Brenda Dawson, still living in the village, and it is thanks to the memories of Brenda and her sister Barbara Wilshere that we know something about their Uncle Joseph.

The French family seem always to have lived near the pond in the Little Green area of the village and at some point moved into Holly Tree Cottages, which were probably owned by the Gurneys of Elm Tree Farm. Their home was one of the two small cottages since converted into one, lying just on the right in Hambridge Way. However, at that time, the track which had been used for centuries as a route to Hitchin was known as Millway, leading to the mill at Oughton Head.

The inevitability of the war must have been a major topic in Joseph's conversations with his mates, perhaps over a pint in the Shoulder of Mutton pub, just a short distance from his home. Joseph, together with Arthur Castle the father of Brenda and Barbara, enlisted in Hitchin on 4th August 1914, one of the first Pirton recruits. Joseph's enlistment celebrated, to the day, the 25th anniversary of his baptism. How Pirton and the world had changed in that time! Joseph became Private 14223 of 1st Battalion Bedfordshire Regiment and, together with Brenda's father, was serving in France two months later. He may well have had a short leave home, but he was certainly in France again in May 1915.

Some months on, news came back home that Joseph had been wounded, but no detail followed from the War Office. So Kate, Joe's older sister by six years, wrote to the government officials, receiving a reply that the wound was only slight, and he had returned to duty. The following April, 1916, he was home on leave, later described by his parents as *'In good spirits and keen on his soldier duties.'* They also said that he regularly wrote home, always *'In a cheerful and plucky vein'*. The last time he wrote was a field card received on 26th August. In just over a week he was dead.

It is probable that Joseph spent all this time in France. The huge offensive which became known as the Battle of the Somme had already claimed the life of a younger Pirton man, Frank Handscombe; it would be the scene of other Pirton deaths. It is likely that he was in the Bedfords' advance on 27th July against Delville Wood, adjacent to the village of Longueval, which continued as the scene of intense and prolonged fighting. At the centre of the battle at

British troops observing from a trench near Thiepval. The only scene – desolation.

Delville Wood was a South African brigade who went in with 3,000 men, of whom less than 800 emerged unscathed.

The 1st Bedfords continued in heavy fighting and, on 3rd September, they captured Wedge Wood and part of the Battalion reached Ginchy, although that was not to fall until later. In the morass which the battle had become, we cannot tell the whereabouts of Joseph; attempts to dislodge the Germans and personal survival were the orders of the day.

Sadly, survival soon came to an end for many of these frightened, but heroic men. Monday 4th September, a day with low clouds and showers throughout, was a bad one for the British Army with 669 men killed on that single day. In the 1st Bedfordshire Regiment alone, Private Joseph French and 39 other men died; 15 men the day before and 23 the following day.

The story of Joseph's death, passed down through the family, was that after receiving a minor wound, he was attending a first aid post when a German shell made a direct hit and all within the First Aid post were killed. However, some recent research seems more accurate. It relates that a Private Kilbey wrote to his sister, asking her to let Joseph's mother know how her son died. '*Pte J French was going over the parapet of a trench with an attack, when a bullet entered the centre of his forehead and he was killed instantly*'. Pte Kilbey went on to write that he visited the grave where his pal was buried.

It seems that Private Joseph French was buried in a military cemetery, which was later fought over and the graves destroyed. His family searched for a long while to find his burial place and Barbara, Joseph's niece, remembers her grandparents speaking of Thiepval. Indeed, it is at the huge and awe-inspiring Thiepval *'Memorial for the Missing'* that Joseph's name is commemorated (Pier & Face 2C I); one of 73,367 men who died in a relatively small area of the Somme and have no known grave. It is a monument which commemorates a further Pirton loss, six days later.

On hearing of his death, Joseph's father, William French, wrote in the family Bible, *'Joseph dide in France, September 4th, aged 27'*(sic). Brenda and Barbara well remember an 'award' presented to their grandparents, a memorial medal consisting of a circular copper disc bearing the words *'He died for Freedom and Honour'*. This was given to the relatives of all who lost their lives in the Great War; it became known as the *'Dead Man's Penny'*.

Joseph's mother died in 1931 and his father in 1935; both are buried in Pirton St. Mary's churchyard.

Carved into the stone of the Thiepval 'Memorial to the Missing' are the names of more than 72,000 United Kingdom and South African soldiers who died in the Somme and have no known grave. Most of them died between July and November 1916.

One of these names is Private Joseph French from Pirton. Fellow villager, Private Raymond Jenkins, killed six days later, is also commemorated on this magnificent Monument.

Soldier 5: Died Sunday 10th September 1916

PRIVATE JOHN PARSELL

WITH PIRTON MATES AS A SHELL KILLS HIM

He was just a lad, only 18; the youngest Pirton man to die in the war. No matter how many deaths occurred in the conflict, the thought of such a young country boy perishing in the mud and blood of the Somme, touches a very raw nerve. John Frederick Parsell was the third Pirton man to die on that tragic battlefield. At the time of his death he was with two village mates, one of whom died a week later from wounds received from the same shell. Private John Parsell was, in fact, killed on the same day as another Pirton soldier, in a different part of the Somme – Private Ray Jenkins.

Young John came from a family that moved around a great deal in Hertfordshire. His father, also John, was an itinerant worker and whilst born in rural Hertfordshire, as a young man he lived in north London working at Hornsey Gas Works. John Senior was married, first to Elizabeth who may well have died in an unfulfilled pregnancy, and then to Sarah, mother of his three children. It was with this family that he moved around Hertfordshire for employment which was increasingly difficult to find.

Young John had two older siblings; William born in Benington and Katherine in Stapleford, both small Hertfordshire villages. The family then moved to Stotfold, just over the border in Bedfordshire, where John was born in early 1898. By his third birthday the family was living in Aston, not far from his father's birthplace. Still in North Hertfordshire, they then moved between Holwell and Great Green in Pirton; for a short spell living near Walnut Tree Farm (now part of nos. 23-25 Walnut Tree Road). The Pirton link strengthened with John at the village school where he made many friends, some of whom later shared the same trench with him at the Front.

Leaving school, he worked in Timothy White's

chemist shop in the market square in Hitchin. He is recorded as *'Having done his work thoroughly and his painstaking ways won the admiration of those who knew him well'*.

Along with some of his Pirton mates, John, just sixteen, joined the Herts Territorials in February 1914. The evenings he spent with the 'Terriers' in Hitchin provided an exciting change from his rather mundane working day. As John and his mates walked down Millway to Hitchin, much of the conversation was about joining the 'real' army and having a *'go at the Hun'*. It was from Pirton that he soon enlisted as Private John Frederick Parsell, no. 1366, 1st Battalion Hertfordshire Regiment. By the end of August, thirty two Pirton men, including the group of former school friends who were with the Herts Territorials, had joined up; all listed on the Vicar's new *'Roll of Honour'*.

Even before the outbreak of the Great War, John was well into military training, but owing to his youth he did not go to France until July 1915. He would have been bitterly disappointed when some

In the peaceful pre-1914 days, John Parsell worked at Timothy Whites in the market square of Hitchin.

of his Pirton mates went to the Front without him in 1914.

Christmas 1914, found John in camp at Hertford writing home, *'I am very happy and comfortable and getting on well. I wish everyone a happy Christmas'*. The following July, still only seventeen and a half years old, he was sent to France, but nothing is known of his early movements there. In the particularly bitter February of 1916 he had a short leave in Pirton. No doubt he enquired of his many friends who were away serving; his home visit coincided with the news of the first death of a Pirton man, Company Sergeant Major Frank Cannon.

By September of that year, the war was continuing its ghastly course and the new secret weapon of the British army - the tank - rolled into action on the western front, stunning the Germans but proving very unreliable. The Herts regiment was in the 118th Brigade of the 39th Division, the main body of which attacked north of the River Ancre on 3rd September; the Herts in reserve.

He had been in a makeshift hospital suffering from an unknown illness, but returned to the Front on the 9th September. The following day, yet another one overcast with rain, was a bad one for the British. 651 British losses were recorded on the Western Front and within a few hours of returning to his regiment, 18 year old John Parsell was killed. He was the first of the Pirton men in the Herts Regiment *'To make the great sacrifice of giving his life for the Country'*. On that fateful day, John was with two other Pirton colleagues when, in a barrage of German shells, he was killed. In the same explosion the two other Pirton men, Privates George Roberts and Arthur Walker, were wounded.

A local paper wrote of Private John Parsell in the chilling words of the time: *'A kind-hearted son, full of patriotic pride for his country...we hope the villagers will feel proud of the noble sacrifice he has made for his Country'*. To Sarah and John Parsell the death of their youngest son, still only eighteen, must simply have been a heart-breaking loss.

The dreadful matter of writing the letter to inform his parents of their son's death rested with two Pirton men. Corporal Harry Smith, who was suffering from major battle shock, passed the task to Pte. Edward Goldsmith. We can imagine the news from the war-torn trenches arriving in a seemingly peaceful Pirton and, in a moment, tearing the life of his family apart. The letter, written the day after John's death, read:

'I now commence the most regrettable duty I have - to inform you that John was killed yesterday afternoon. It may be small consolation to you to know that his death was

practically instantaneous. I was only about twenty yards from him at the time the shell burst. I can assure you he suffered no pain.'

The deep sense of comradeship, which had transferred from Pirton to the Western Front, was well expressed in the next part of the letter: *'He was very cheerful, having just seen Fred Baines and Arthur Odell in the Royal Sussex (both to die in 1918), and George Thompson'* (All were Pirton men). The two Pirton men wounded at the same time as John Parsell were on their way back to England, but Arthur Walker later died of his wounds.

> *'We have just been out of the trenches to the burial of the dead. It was most touching to us, being such close comrades. I can only say the loss of John will be felt very keenly.'*

The letter concludes by saying that when Pte Goldsmith returns to Pirton he would bring for John's mother, *'One or two little articles'* that were in her son's kit.

Private John Parsell was buried at the Knightsbridge Cemetery, Mesnil-Martinsart in France (Ref F. 28). A few days later the Revd. Erskine William Langmore made a touching reference to Pte. John Parsell's death during a Sunday service at St. Mary's, Pirton. He is one of the five Pirton men on the Hertfordshire Territorials' Memorial at their Hitchin headquarters; he is also on the Hitchin War Memorial.

One of his closest friends who had been at school with him and enlisted at the same time wrote a tribute:

> *'Sleep on in your peace in that unknown grave,*
> *For you fought and died, when your years were best;*
> *You left all you loved to sail o'er the wave,*
>
> *You fought the good fight, then were called to rest.*
>
> *Sweet memory now lives in the heart.*
> *Of your mother, who mourns for her boy;*
> *With the hope to meet and never to part*
> *In peace of eternal joy.'*

PIRTON'S YOUNG TERRIERS

John Parsell was one of the young men from Pirton who joined the Hitchin Territorials well before the Great War began. He was the first of six to die.

This Memorial at the Hitchin Territorials Headquarters honours the Terriers from the Herts Regiment who died, including John Parsell*.

*Parsell has been used as the spelling of the family name, as it is on the Pirton War Memorial and as recorded by the Commonwealth War Graves Commission. On the Hitchin War Memorials and in some newspapers the surname is spelt as Parcell.

Soldier 6: Died Sunday 10th September 1916

PRIVATE (ALFRED) RAYMOND JENKINS

PIRTON'S 'BIG FELLOW': ANOTHER VICTIM OF THE SOMME

At the village school he was known as the *'big fellow'* and at 6ft. 1½ inches it was no surprise when he joined the Grenadier Guards, the only Pirton man to do so. Alfred Raymond Jenkins was born and lived in Pirton and like a number of other village lads at the turn of the century, moved away from labouring in the fields to working on the railway. Whilst christened with his father's name, he was always known by his second Christian name. Like several of his village mates, he was killed during the 141 days of the Battle of the Somme

His father, born in Stondon, married Elvina Reynolds in 1887; she was a Pirton lass whose family had lived in the village for several generations. They made their home in a farm-owned cottage in the Little Green area of the village known then as Silver Street, later as Royal Oak Lane. Alfred worked as a bricklayer throughout his life and whether in the village or further afield there was plenty of work to call on his trade. Alfred and Elvina (sometimes referred to as Elizabeth) had at least ten children of whom two, Arthur and Alice, died in infancy. The surviving sons were: Montague, Alfred Raymond, Edward, Leonard, Geoffrey, John and Norman. Emma, the sole surviving daughter, was their youngest child. Their second son, Alfred Raymond, later known simply as Ray, was born on 4th April 1895.

Children were young when they started at the village school in those days and Ray was only three years and five months old when he was admitted to the Infant School. Just coming up to his eighth birthday he moved into the 'big school', officially known as the Pirton Board Mixed School. He was already a tall lad and seemed to have been an industrious pupil, working hard and in May 1908 left the school having gained his 'Proficiency Certificate'.

St. Mary's Church was a major influence in Pirton, certainly so with the Jenkins family. Most of the village children attended the Methodist Chapel or St. Mary's, with a smaller number at the Baptist Chapel. Ten year-old Ray Jenkins regularly attended St. Mary's Sunday School, sang in the choir and conducted himself well; his parents gave much support to the Church, too. The family not only gave financially to the building of a south transept at St. Mary's, but Ray's father, being a builder, gave freely of his talents to help with the roofing and internal plastering. This addition to St. Mary's, built entirely by village efforts, was dedicated in July 1914.

For this tall, relatively well educated thirteen year old lad, career choices were better than for many. He started as an engine cleaner and at the outbreak of the war, was a railway employee probably working at Hitchin Station on the Midland Line. The railway system was still expanding and provided employment for many local men. It is likely that Ray was one of

Hitchin railway station

the many that walked from the village, down Millway (now known as Hambridge Way) to the market town of Hitchin, a centre of work for an increasing number of Pirton villagers.

Whilst this *'big fellow'* was probably enjoying his work with the railway and there was no compulsion to join up, the pressures on him, not least from some of his old school mates and maybe his own conscience, caused him to give a week's notice to his railway employers in June 1915. With his height, relatively unusual a century ago, it was natural that he should be posted into the Grenadier Guards; in Ray's case the 1st Battalion, regimental number 24100.

A year after joining up he was sent to France. Whilst his movements are not known during this time, we do know that he *'wrote home cheerfully'* and in that late summer, perhaps with a smile on his face, asked for some Christmas pudding to be sent out. *'There's nothing like asking in plenty of time'*, he wrote. His father had died early in 1914 (He never saw the completion of St. Mary's south transept that he had helped build) and his mother had moved from Pirton to Brampton Cottage in Brampton Park Road Hitchin. Life must have been very hard for her with four children still at home, but she kept herself busy writing to her four sons who were in the armed forces. Ray was also a considerable letter writer. In the summer of 1916, whilst he was attached to an entrenchment battalion, he wrote home to the local War Comfort Fund, thanking them for a parcel of cigarettes he received on 24th August. *'Woodbines are the general favourite, hard to come by and the parcel from Hitchin jolly fine'*.

Wednesday 6th September 1916 found Ray and some twenty of his mates, including Pirton soldier Private Sid Smith, resting in a barn not far from the Front. They had been in the trenches for many days, and he knew he would soon have to return. It was here that he wrote what was to be his final letter home. He was not far from the two small villages of Guillemont and Ginchy; both completely destroyed where *'Not a stick or stone is to be seen. Not a tree stands.'*

Four days later, 10th September, under leaden

skies, one company of the 1st Battalion of the Grenadiers went forward to Arrow Head Copse in support of the 4th Battalion of the Grenadiers and the 1st Welsh Guards, the latter coming into action against an enemy attack. On that day, fifty one men from the Grenadier Guards were killed in fierce fighting; Private Alfred Raymond Jenkins was one of them.

Like so many others, including his older Pirton school mate Joseph French, Ray has no known grave and is remembered on the Thiepval Memorial to the '*Missing in France*'. (Pier/Face 8D). Two young men, both born in Pirton, baptised at St. Mary's, attending the village school, killed within six days of each other on the terrible battlefields of the Somme and both commemorated at the awesome and magnificently tragic Thiepval Memorial.

Even amid the unbelievable carnage, some of his chums managed to send a postcard along the trenches to other friends, to tell them that '*Poor old Ray Jenkins*' had been killed. This was recorded by Pte F Adams, also in the Guards, in a letter to his wife living in West Alley Hitchin. In the Great War the four battalions of the Grenadier Guards fought in all the principle battles of the Western Front, suffering 12,000 casualties.

As the war moved towards an anticipated conclusion, Pirton people wanted to see beyond their tears and honour the fallen. Names were put forward for an intended Memorial. Initially nineteen names were submitted, but Ray's name was missing; his widowed mother had moved to Hitchin and, maybe, she was unaware of the memorial being considered. Later, his name and ten others, including those still to die in the last three months of the war were added. His name is also on the Hitchin War Memorial.

In 1916, a song picking up on the natural beauty of Picardy, where the Battle of the Somme took place, proved instantly popular and was sung by many men who had left loved ones behind.

> '*Roses are shining in Picardy,*
> *In the hush of the silvery dew.*
> *Roses are flowering in Picardy,*
> *But there's never a rose like you!*'

Yet its sentimental lyrics did not fully conceal all the realities of that time and place:

> '*And the roses will die with the summertime,*
> *And our hearts may be far apart,*
> *But there's one rose that dies not in Picardy!*
> *'Tis the rose that I keep in my heart!*'

St. Mary's Church (1905). Ray Jenkins attended Sunday School and sang in the choir, his family worshipped and his father helped build the south transept.

Soldier 7: Died Monday 18th September 1916

PRIVATE ARTHUR WALKER

LEAVES A WIFE AND CHILD AFTER DYING FROM WOUNDS

The way in which families were interwoven in Pirton ninety years ago formed a giant village network; not least as marriage between cousins was quite common. So, when news of a casualty came through, many relatives were affected; families previously living a quiet existence were suddenly torn apart by what was happening in a foreign country. This was never more so than with Arthur Walker, who was with some Pirton mates when wounded by a shell, dying of his injuries eight days later.

Arthur was born on 13th November 1892. He was the youngest of seven children of George Walker, a farm labourer, and Sarah (nee Odell) who, like many, added to the modest family income by strawplaiting. The family lived in Bury End, the home of their granddaughter ninety years later. Their first born child, John, died when he was fifteen.

On leaving school, Arthur worked on a local farm. His mother, Sarah, died in 1907 and his father moved away to work. By 1911, Arthur was sharing their Bury End cottage with his brother Herbert and sister, Gertrude.

In 1915, he married Rose Males; they had been together at the village school. Her parents, George and Annis Males, lived in a cottage near The Fox (now part of no. 41 High Street) and kept the Old Hall pub (now Docwra Manor). The marriage ceremony in St. Mary's did not pass without its moments! The Vicar wrote in the parish magazine, under the heading *'A Disgrace to Pirton'*:

> *'The conduct of some at the wedding on November 22nd was disgraceful. They showed respect neither for God's Acre nor God's House and seemed to come for merriment instead of attendance at a solemn service.'*

Arthur had enlisted in the village in 1914 as Private 2364 in the 1st Battalion, Hertfordshire Regiment. He was one of the 'Pirton Terriers' and had gone to the Front in November 1914. A month later he wrote home, thanking the villagers for a jersey and other things he had just received.

> *'Best things you could have sent... I can't get about much as I've got frozen feet, half the battalion are laid up with it. Please put packet of fag papers in the next parcel. It's hard to get anything here, bar cold hands and feet.'*

In early October, one of Arthur's mates wrote home to say that they had been through two great battles which were *'nothing less than hell'*. They had been in the firing line for thirty-six days with only one day out. However, he added that *'The Pirton lads are OK'*.

By the beginning of 1916, all four Walker brothers were fighting for their country; Frederick with the 11th Hussars, Sidney the Artillery, Herbert and Arthur with the 1st Hertfordshire Regiment. Herts G Company was a closely-knit regiment, made up from the old Hitchin and Stevenage Companies and with several Pirton men who had known each other since their schooldays. They had already fought together through terrible times, almost certainly in May 1915 when the regiment was in the attack around Festubert, with the British suffering some 16,000 casualties. The following September found them at Loos, marked by the use of poison gas, by the British for the first time.

Maybe, the Pirton Vicar would have excused the *'disgraceful behaviour'* at Arthur's wedding had he known the horrors that Arthur and his mates had faced and to which they would quickly return. Harry Smith, who had been Arthur's best man at the wedding described by the Vicar in such a disapproving tone, was killed in 1917.

In October 1915, Arthur, along with other Pirton

Bury End and Great Green, a small and close community, was home for Arthur Walker and five other men killed in the Great War. It must have been a place of much shared grief.

mates, was rocked by the news of the death of a close friend, Private Herbert John Clarke from nearby Offley. He had ten young children. How much Arthur had told Rose about his war experiences on his wedding leave is unknown. The last thing he wanted was to cause her great anxiety. Of Christmas 1915 he wrote:

> *'We were happy all the time; and had a good sing-song to keep the Germans in good spirits, for they could easily hear us, as their trenches were only twenty yards away in one place. But the Germans were careful not to show their heads for us to get a shot at them.'*

He continued:

> *'(The Company) are all alive and kicking and in the best of health. We can all think ourselves lucky to be in good health after being in so much mud and water for eight days.'*

'Lucky' would hardly seem a word for the awful circumstances in which the men were living at the Front.

In May 1916, he had a short leave, probably the last time he saw Rose. As the summer moved on the two armies became ever more locked in dreadful battle, with just a few yards gained counting as a major victory. The Battle of the Somme stretched over four and a half months.

The weather in September matched the mood of the time; cold, depressing and wet. On the 3rd September it is likely that Arthur was engaged in the attack north of the River Ancre. By the 10th, he was in some of the fiercest fighting along with other Pirton men, including George Roberts and John Parsell. On that day, G Company came under heavy fire and one of a barrage of shells killed Pte John Parsell, wounding Privates George Roberts and Arthur Walker. George Roberts' injuries were serious, though not life-threatening, and he was transferred to King George's Hospital in London. The wounds to Arthur were to prove fatal - but not for eight days. Sometime after 10th September, Private

Goldsmith, another Pirton man, writing home said that he didn't know what had happened to the wounded Arthur Walker, *'As when he left the trenches everything was in a state of confusion'*.

It is not known whether the letter telling Rose of Arthur's injuries reached her before or after his death. Ironically, the Rev E J Welsher, chaplain of the French hospital which received Arthur, wrote:

'Dear Mrs Walker, Your husband was brought in wounded yesterday and he thinks you might worry until you hear, so he has asked me to write and so relieve your mind. He has asked me to say you have no need to worry, that he is doing quite well. Of course, he is feeling bad, but as far as we can see there is nothing serious, so we trust that all will be well. I hope that he will soon be well enough to travel, and that you will have the pleasure and joy of seeing him, as he longs to get home.'

This well-intended letter from the regimental chaplain, which was dated the 11th September, was written rather too quickly; for Arthur's condition worsened and he died seven days later. Further confusion followed when a local paper wrote that he was killed by *'gun-shot wounds in the shoulder, head and wrist'*.

However, there is little doubt that he died from the shell wounds that killed his mate John Parsell. Private Arthur Walker died from his wounds eight days later, on Monday 18th September 1916, in one of the many large hospitals around Boulogne. He was 23 and was buried at the Boulogne Eastern Cemetery, Pas de Calais, France, Ref. VIII. C. 143. He is one of the five Pirton men on the Hertfordshire Territorials' Memorial at their Hitchin headquarters.

And so in his home village the many intertwined families - the Walkers, Davies, Males, Odells, Baines and others - lost a dear relative, others a close friend. Rose, aged 23 was left a widow with a young son, Stanley who was born in March 1915; Arthur will only have seen him as a baby.

Arthur's three brothers - Frederick, Sidney and Herbert all survived the war. Some time later, Rose married Arthur's brother, Herbert, and they lived on in the village. Stanley, the only child of Arthur and Rose, lived in Pirton with his wife Mabel and two sons until the last few years of his life.

**The destruction became worse with each passing day of the war.
This picture shows the scene at Pys, a French village.**

Soldier 8: Died Monday 13th November 1916

PRIVATE SIDNEY BAINES

FAMILY'S ADDED GRIEF AT NEVER KNOWING HIS BURIAL PLACE

To lose a husband or a son when he is only 24 is a tragic loss, but what made the death of Sidney Baines even worse was that neither his widow, nor parents ever knew where he was buried; closure of their grief was never complete.

To visit Pirton and see today's affluent village makes it hard to understand the simplicity, indeed the hardship of Sidney's family and most others at the beginning of the twentieth century. The small two up and two down cottages have been extended, some pulled down and replaced; people now commute to London, no longer to the surrounding fields. Until 1980, where nos. 7-13 Shillington Road now stand, was a row of cottages. They were popularly known as 'Ten Steps' and had been built in the mid 18th century; in the second of this row of cottages, lived the Baines family. The parents, Albert and Emma Elizabeth (known as Elizabeth), both came from Pirton families and would rarely have seen beyond this small part of the North Hertfordshire countryside. From their union came five boys and five girls of whom one, Ida, died in infancy. The fourth child, Sidney (sometimes spelt as Sydney) was born on 27th March 1892, and just over two decades later he was jettisoned into the hell-hole called the Somme where he was killed in 1916.

Like many cottages in the village, the Baines' house was a crowded one. Lily, one of the younger family members, recalled how their home *'Seemed so full, that armed with my bread, egg and mattress I would go each evening to my older sister's house by the pond to sleep'*.

Sidney left the village school in 1906 and started work on one of the local farms. His older brother Charlie was a coachbuilder and wheelwright and this may have persuaded Sidney to look beyond village for employment. Sometime after 1911 he found work in the nearby Garden City at Letchworth Woodworking. This was a short-lived job and he moved on to Phoenix Motors Ltd, a company which manufactured light cars at their Pixmore Avenue factory in the new Garden City.

With the outbreak of the war, some of Pirton's more adventurous young men immediately enlisted, but Sidney did not join up until 9th February 1916. This well-built, young man enlisted at Bedford, becoming Private Baines, 26026 of the 4th Battalion, Bedfordshire Regiment.

The villages of Pirton and Shillington may be separated by a county border, but they lie only two miles apart, and those looking for a marriage partner outside Pirton looked first to Shillington. Sidney's heart was captured by lass of his own age, Ethel Lily (Bunyan) who worked at The Grange in Shillington.

They were married early in 1916 and a daughter, Edna Joan, was born on 3rd June 1916. It is likely

A Letchworth Garden City factory for manufacturing Phoenix Cars was Sidney Baines' workplace shortly before he joined up in 1916.

that Sidney saw her, albeit briefly, just before his regiment was shipped across the Channel and landed at Le Havre on 25th July 1916.

He was soon to be in the Battle of the Somme where the carnage was measured in thousands. It seems almost certain that Sidney was with his regiment on 11th November as they were moved yet again towards the Front, eventually reaching Puchevillers just after midday and proceeding on to Varennes the next day around 2.30pm. The day was one of low cloud and mist with patches of fog obliterating anything more than a short distance away. The landscape which had once been of small farms and fields had, over a long period of fighting and progressively greater fire-power, become a sea of desolation with roads churned up into an endless quagmire. Movement became increasingly difficult as the terrain deteriorated, yet Sidney and his colleagues kept slogging on and on. In places the line of troops waded knee-deep in mud and some men were even drowned in those foul-smelling and rat-infested places.

Each trench had been given a name and the 4th Bedfords marched to assembly trenches off *'Bedford Street'* and *'Victoria Street'*. Here they took up position prior to mounting an attack between Beaumont Hamel and the right bank of the River Ancre which, some five miles south reached Albert, known simply as *'Bert'* by the Tommies. Vera Brittain visiting this town three years after the end of the war, describing it *'as a humped ruin of stones and dust'*.

This was the boundary of the German lines which saw the enemy in a particularly strong defensive position. The battle for Beaumont-Hamel and Beaumont-sur-l'ancre, originally planned for October had been postponed several times due to unfavourable weather conditions. As preparation for the battle took place, the men had to contend with the dangers of gas and high explosives from the Germans. The long planned military offensive thus took place between 13th and 19th November. This was to be the fourth phase of the Battle of the Somme, a momentous attack.

For Sidney and all the men in this sector, the morning of the 13th was again foggy and abnormally dark. It was greeted by a great barrage of British guns, the precursor of the men advancing through appalling conditions and hampered by all they had to carry. The advance started at 6.45am and during the next few hours heavy casualties were sustained. The day was a bad one for Sidney's regiment with fourteen officers and 48 other ranks killed, 108 wounded and a further sixteen posted missing. There came a danger, too, from the air, as German aircraft became a growing threat with their bombing, albeit primitive compared with more recent warfare.

Sometime during that day of mud, bullets, shells and slaughter, Sidney was killed. He joined the ever growing number who would never return to their homes and

British troops crossing a muddy area in the Ancre Valley in October 1916.

loved ones. Some two weeks later the Battle of the Somme faded, four months after the offensive began. Over half a million allies were killed, a number well exceeded by German fatalities. A.A. Milne, later to seek solace in writing the stories of Christopher Robin and Pooh Bear, was in another part of the British line during these dreadful November days and described it all as a *'nightmare of mental and moral degradation'*.

Following the German withdrawal in the spring of 1917, this battlefield was cleared and a number of cemeteries created, of which Ancre British Cemetery was one. The majority of those buried in the cemetery died on 1st July, 3rd September or 13th November 1916; Sidney on the last of these days. The cemetery was located on what was once No Man's Land during those closing stages of the Somme offensive. Sidney lies buried there. (Ref. I. C. 26)

News of his death reached England slowly. Sidney's wife, Ethel, was told on 6th December that he had been *'missing'* since 13th November. This was confirmed by Private Gadger of Shillington although Private Stapleton from nearby Holwell said that he was killed on that day. He was officially posted as *'missing'*, but when official confirmation of his death reached Ethel is not known. The sixth Pirton man killed in the 141 bloody days of the Battle of the Somme.

Sidney left a young widow and daughter he had, at best, seen very briefly. The grief for his widow and parents, Albert and Elizabeth, was made worse by the fact that they never knew where he was buried. Many years passed before members of this large family learnt of his final resting place.

Sidney's widow later married Bert Elms and they lived at Pirton Grange; she, like the rest of the family, just had to get on with her life. Sidney's daughter Edna married and with her mother, moved to Luton. Sylvia, a granddaughter of Sidney, still lives in that area.

When he was 70, Sidney's father Albert took on the job of village roadman and became known as *'the little man with the big broom'*. He kept the village roads immaculate and if an accident occurred on the Hitchin road he cut a cross on the grass verge as mark of respect. He must often have wished that he could place such a cross on his son's grave.

Albert Baines

Soldier 9: Died Thursday 21st December 1916

PRIVATE EDWARD CHARLES BURTON
KILLED FOUR DAYS SHORT OF HIS 20th BIRTHDAY

It should have been such a special Christmas. He was born on Christmas Day and would have celebrated his twentieth birthday. Not a lavish celebration, for he was of modest means; maybe a family party, maybe a drink with his mates. Sadly, it was not to be, for just four days before that 20th birthday, he was killed in a foreign country.

By the late autumn of 1916 the knowledge that eight Pirton men had been killed in the war, cast a cloud of great sadness and anxiety over the closely-knit community of Pirton.

How different the village had been twenty years earlier in the tranquil days when Edward Charles Burton was born. His mother Ellen Burton, born in 1874, was the daughter of the wonderfully named Goliath Burton and his first wife, Mary-Ann. Ellen's husband-to-be, George Pearce, was from a poorer family, but whilst life was hard for the young couple, it was a time of peacefulness.

Ellen was living with her parents in what is now Crabtree House and George lived up the Baulk in a cottage, later burnt down. Ellen went to the village school and proved a good scholar, but George never had the opportunity to read or write, and at the age of seven he was working on the land, scaring birds off the nearby fields. He later became stockman at High Down Farm.

From an early age Edward Charles, the first-born to Ellen and George, was known as Charlie; arriving on Christmas Day 1896. A short time later, Ellen and George married at Woolwich. *'I don't know why they got married there'*, their youngest and only surviving daughter Phyllis Pearce said recently, *'but I've got their wedding certificate to show just that'*. It may have been that for a few years George worked at Beckdon gasworks in Woolwich, but this is far from certain. Once married, they moved to a cottage now part of 69 High Street; subsequently moving to the end cottage in Holwell Road (now no. 24).

Charlie was to have six siblings: Francis John (Jack), Frederick, Lillian, Stanley Goliath, Laurence and finally Phyllis who was born in 1913. Charlie, born before his parents' marriage, had been christened, and retained, his mother's maiden name – Burton. All his siblings, born after the parents' marriage, carried their father's surname, Pearce.

Charlie was born in, and continued to live at his grandparents' house in Crabtree Lane and referred to Grandfather Goliath's house as *'my home'*.

Crabtree House

Goliath Burton's third wife Charlotte (nee Weeden) whom he married in 1905, continued to live in the same farmhouse and after Goliath's death four years into their marriage, was a major influence when Charlie left school and worked on the family's substantial smallholding in the village. After Goliath's death it was his son Herbert for whom Charlie worked. Charlie still lived with his grandmother at Crabtree House, with just a young servant, Ethel Handscombe. However, this work was all interrupted when, like so many of his former school friends, he answered the call of *'King and Country'*. This slim, extremely youthful looking man became Private E C Burton, 28050, of the 2nd Battalion Bedfordshire Regiment, enlisting in Bedford. At a later stage he became a member of the machine gun section.

Detail of his early army life is unknown, but it is fortunate that his youngest sister, now 95-year old Phyllis Pearce, can talk about the family. However, she was only three when Charlie was killed and has no personal memory of him.

Sometime in the summer of 1916, Charlie made the journey across the Channel; a short distance, but one to a truly different world. War had long been raging along the Western Front, but with no real consequence other than the deaths of many men. Just south of the war-torn Arras to Doullens Road lay the village of Berles-au-Bois. It was in and around Berles that Charlie was to spend the final months of his life.

In mid July 1916, the 2nd Bedfords attacked south of Trones Alley where the Germans had a stronghold in a wood. The attack was slowed down by massive gunfire and the allied forces were pushed back except for a small wedge on the western side of the wood occupied by a small party of the Bedfords. On 30th July, Charlie was almost certainly involved in another major attack; this time the objective was Faffemont Farm. The day started with early morning fog and the stench of high explosive and gas shells from German guns. The 2nd Bedfords attacked from the west, but it was not until early September that the farm was finally taken. Uncut barbed wire and massive German gunfire had held up progress and caused even more casualties.

The summer gave way to autumn, the only recognisable difference being the fall in temperatures; adding even greater hardship to the mud, gunfire and bloodshed. That autumn, there was no fall of leaves. *'There was no trees left intact at all, just stumps and treetops and barbed wire all mixed up together, and bodies all over the place. Jerries and ours,'* it was recorded.

During November, Charlie was billeted in the village of Berles-au-Bois. At the beginning of December the weather worsened and whilst the hard frost enabled easier movement over the muddy surface, the cold bit into every part of the body. Sleet followed and then falls of snow.

The *'anonymous'* soldiers, like Charlie Burton, faced this unforgiving war alongside the famous. One of these was the Major JWHT Douglas, an Olympic boxing champion at the 1908 Games and later to become a household name after the war when he captained the England cricket team.

Christmas was drawing ever closer and the 2nd Bedfords' war diary reveals the last days of Private Charlie Burton's young life:

17 Dec 1916 Trenches BERLES. Casualties Nil. A quiet day.
18 Dec 1916 Trenches BERLES. Casualties Nil. .
19 Dec 1916 Trenches BERLES. Casualties Nil.
20 Dec 1916 Trenches BERLES. Casualties Nil.
21 Dec 1916 Trenches BERLES. Casualties 2 O.R. Killed 4 O.R. Wounded

Charlie was with a machine gun section of the Bedfords and was one of the two other ranks to be killed on 21st December, ironically whilst '*taking a break for tea*'. Additional to the official letter, the news of the young soldier's death was conveyed by another Pirton man, stretcher-bearer Pte. Charles Furr, in a letter to his wife.

The Times newspaper recorded 1916 as '*the bleakest Christmas yet*'. If the tragic news got back to Pirton quickly it must have been a particularly joyless Christmas for Ellen and George, Charlotte and the other members of the large Burton clan. The year's most popular song, *'Take me back to dear old Blighty'* must have had a bitter ring for the Burton and Pearce families.

Ellen and George were two more parents who thought that their son had never had a burial place. In fact, he is buried at Berles Position Military Cemetery (Ref B1), some fifteen kilometres south-west of Arras. A long grassy path leads to this small, beautiful cemetery which lies in a peaceful valley; in summer surrounded by fields of golden corn.

After Phyllis had spoken about her brother, she took out the beautiful, so emotive, photograph of her brother's grave which her cousins, Rita and Jack Pearce, had given her. Along with Pirton's War Memorial, the headstone reveals the courage and death of this Pirton man.

Tragically, the loss of their eldest son Charles was not the end of the wartime grief for Ellen and George. Less than two years later another son, Jack, was to become a further name to be recorded on Pirton's War Memorial.

The grave of Private Edward Charles Burton.

Soldier 10: Died Monday 26th February 1917

PRIVATE HARRY CRAWLEY

1917: ANOTHER YEAR – ANOTHER DEATH

By the end of 1916, as statesmen and generals continued to blunder, nine young men from Pirton had already died in the bloodiest war in history. In the next twenty-two months, the number of Pirton casualties was to treble. Torn from the peaceful Pirton, some of these men had volunteered in the euphoria of Kitchener's appeal that *'Your Country Needs You'*; others were conscripted as the numbers of dead at the Front continued to escalate.

Of some of the thirty men listed on Pirton's First World War Memorial much is known, of others precious little. Harry Crawley was typical of millions who died in the Great War, known only in their home villages during peace, in the trenches during the war and on memorials in death. So little is known about Harry Crawley but, as with all our war dead, it is important to record even a largely anonymous story. But, for the reader, anonymity should never obscure these men's emotions; these soldiers from many nations all thought, felt, loved and feared. Sadly, Harry Crawley's thoughts, feelings, loves and fears are not known; only our imagination dwelling on the horrors of this war can provide an image, and that an imperfect one.

For many years Middle Farm was an essential part of Pirton. Until its demolition in 1967, it stood near the heart of the village, where Docklands and some of the newer houses in Crabtree Lane (nos. 14-18) now stand. It was part of the High Down property owned by Priory Estates, and after a fire in the farmyard in 1865, it was divided into two houses. It was into one of these that Henry Charles Crawley (known as Harry) and his young wife Minnie (nee Cherry) lived for most of the time that their son attended the village school.

Harry was their first child, born in late 1881 and christened after his father's nickname. Before young Harry arrived on the scene and during the first years of his life, his father had moved around, although always in North Hertfordshire. Like most Pirton men he was a farm labourer, even at the age of eleven he was working on the land in Offley. But after several moves within Pirton, dependent upon with which farm he was working, Middle Farm became the family home. It was there, opposite St. Mary's Church that Harry thought of as his home, only a short walk to school. His father seems to have found more regular employment as a horse-keeper, probably at High Down Farm.

Whilst the parents struggled to earn enough to survive, their family grew. Harry was the oldest of ten children; and it seems that following his arrival there was Annie (born 1885), Albert

Middle Farm, near St. Mary's Church. It was in a small part of this farm that the Crawley family lived.

Vincent (1886), Florence Rose (1888), Alice (1891), Helen (probably 1892), Milly (1893), Katie (1895), Frank (1896) and Phillip (1902). Many of the older Pirton people remember Phil, whose son Ron has lived in Danefield Road for many years. Also living with the family was Elizabeth Cherry, Harry's maternal grandmother. An important social advance that touched her was the introduction in 1908 of the Old Age Pensions that provided between 1s. and 5s. a week to people over seventy. The sum may seem small, but it meant much to many people in the village.

Certainly within the Crawley family, all the male members seemed destined to work on the land. On leaving school in 1895, young Harry did just that, but by the age of nineteen he, like his father, was a local horse-keeper working for Mr Frank Burton. He moved on with this mainly outdoor work, then moving to Mr Franklin's farm at Walnut Tree Lane. Taking part in a special harvest celebration supper organised by Thomas Franklin in 1911, Harry and other farm-hands added to the merriment with their singing; after all, he had sung in St. Mary's Church choir. One of his mates singing along with him was Fred Anderson, another victim in the not-too-distant war.

Harry did not marry and continued to live in the village. By the time the Great War started, he was 32. He enlisted on the 29th March 1916 and became Private 6539 in one of the Bedfordshire Regiments. With the terrible losses of the war, more and more men were sent to the Front and there were many amalgamations of battalions and the creation of new regiments. Harry was transferred to become Private H. Crawley 33153, of the 6th Battalion, Leicestershire Regiment.

On 6th August 1914, Parliament had sanctioned an increase of half a million men in all ranks of the regular army. Three weeks later, Kitchener asked for another 100,000, called K2. As part of Kitchener's new army, the 6th Battalion was formed at Leicester in August 1914. In April 1915 the Leicestershire men went for training on the bleak Salisbury Plain and on 29th July they embarked for France and Flanders.

Whilst it is uncertain when he was moved to the Leicestershires, Harry was probably with the 6th Leicestershires, part of the 110th Brigade, in the appalling days of the Somme. On 13th July 1916 they were involved in heavy fighting in Mametz Wood, an area that saw terrible casualties. Indeed, a correspondent wrote how a few days previously he saw *'trenches heaped with bodies'*, all British. Dressing stations in hastily erected tents were flooded with casualties and there were many men, some with life-threatening wounds, in the open air waiting their turn for attention. In one small area, seven German machine guns were taken, but not before their sweeping, merciless guns had accounted for many men. At the end of September 1916, men from the same regiment were involved in and around Gueudecourt. On the night of 25th September, the 6th Leicesters attacked a German trench from which much opposition had come, overcame the enemy and held their position. When Gueudecourt was

Private Harry Crawley was taken to one of the many casualty stations near the Front.

finally taken, there were few remains of what had been a pretty village.

Uncertainty surrounds Harry Crawley's part in the foregoing account of men in the Leicestershires, and there is some discrepancy over the date of his death. A local newspaper reports it as 24th February, but we have preferred the date given by the Commonwealth War Graves Commission, namely Monday 26th February 1917. He was shot in the lungs and it seems that death soon followed. Sometimes, one wonders if letters informing the loved ones of men killed are written a little more gently than the actual, awful circumstances of death; if that is so, the sensitivity is to be applauded. Whatever the circumstances, an extract from a letter written by M G C Foley, the sister-in-charge of 33 Casualty Clearing Station in Bethune where Private Harry Crawley died, must have brought some comfort to his mother:

'Your son knew he was dying and was quite conscious to the last. He gave me this message to give to you: "Tell mother that all is well. I am passing peacefully away"'.

His death was just one in a Regiment which was to lose 336 officers and 6692 NCOs and other ranks. He is buried at the Bethune Town Cemetery, Pas de Calais, France. Ref VI.B.75. On his headstone are the words: *"Not my will, but Thine be done"*. The cemetery is the final resting place for men from several nations: 2923 from the United Kingdom, 55 from Canada, 26 from India, 87 from Germany and 122 from France.

Frank, Harry's brother, was in France from September 1916 and was gassed and twice wounded.

Private Harry Crawley's final resting place is in the Bethune Town Cemetery in northern France.

Soldier 11: Died Tuesday 10th April 1917

PRIVATE GEORGE TRUSSELL

THE GULF BETWEEN WAR LEADERS AND THE SOLDIERS

The inevitable gulf between those who ordered the war and those in the trenches is demonstrated all too tragically with Private George Thomas Trussell. George was but one of the thousands reflecting the expendable nature of the soldiers in this war. In such moments of history it is, perhaps, inevitable that politicians and generals are serving the 'big picture' and cannot have easy regard for those sent into battle. George's life, like many, followed a common path: humble roots, enlistment, training and warfare – and all too often, death. Heroes or victims?

On 6th April 1917, a major event to influence the war occurred when President Woodrow Wilson announced that the United States of America had entered the war. Four days later, George Trussell, whose concerns were not with the politics of the war but rather with water-filled trenches, pock-marked landscapes and shells, was killed. Politicians and some senior military leaders were a world away from the soldiers on the battlefield.

Elizabeth Pitts came from a long-established and poor Pirton family. On 6th April 1885 she married a fellow villager, George Trussell. Elizabeth was 28, but their life together in their cottage in 'down-town' Pirton was to be short-lived. Three years later, in April 1888, George died at the early age of 36. Six months after his death, a son to bear his father's name George, was born.

Inter-marriage within Pirton families with the accompanying commonness of village names easily causes confusion in researching the men on our War Memorial. This is well shown by there being two sets of George and Elizabeth Trussells at this time. Between 1881–1893, fourteen children bearing the Trussell name were admitted to the school, probably from five different Trussell families!

Elizabeth gave birth to two children, James and Alice, before she was married; they carried her maiden name. After her marriage she had three more children, George being the youngest. Life for the family must have been hard, desperately so after Elizabeth was left a widow in 1888 whilst

Like this elderly lady, Elizabeth Trussell earned a small income from straw-plaiting; the most common work for village womenfolk – and many children.

all the children were still living at home. She earned only a pittance from straw-plaiting, a situation made worse by an increase in foreign imports driving down the price of plait. The only modest financial relief was that, coinciding with young George going to the village school, fees no longer had to be paid.

It is likely that on leaving school, young George

earned what he could as a farm worker, then moving on to be a stable groom. There is no indication that he married. By the outbreak of the war, he was twenty-six and in the summer of 1916 he enlisted at Hitchin, becoming Private George Trussell G/22199, 6th Battalion, the Queen's (Royal West Surrey) Regiment.

In January 1917 George was almost certainly part of the 6th Battalion which moved to Arras in preparation for a major offensive. The British Army launched this large scale attack as part of a master plan by the new French Commander in Chief, General Robert Nivelle, later to be sacked. Although initially successful, the offensive was soon bogged down, becoming a terribly costly affair. The British attack was against the formidable Hindenburg Line, to which the enemy had recently made a strategic withdrawal. To get through the acres of barbed wire was hellish, never mind the machine gun and cannon fire. It is uncertain in which part of the attack George was involved, for it was a complex offensive and keeping records was far from anyone's mind in the ensuing bloodshed.

On the 9th April, in bitingly cold weather, the battalion was involved in the advance known as *'Easter Egg'* as it took place on Good Friday and Easter Monday. This was part of the attack near Vimy Ridge, made famous through the courage and huge losses of Canadian soldiers. On the previous evening, 8th April, 30,000 members of the Canadian Corps began to move to the front line. Attackers advanced and broke through the first, second and third line of defences, by-passing strong points which were later mopped up. At 5.30 the next morning in driving sleet and to the accompaniment of 2,800 allied guns pounding the German trenches, the British armies emerged from tunnels and trenches. The Canadian infantry went over the top and moved relentlessly towards Vimy Ridge which they took by the middle of that day. George could well have been in one of the advances on either side of Arras and the Scarpe, a river which flows through Arras, all part of this great offensive.

The military leaders had given great thought to the offensive, much had been carefully rehearsed, but it was the men from the trenches whose lives were at risk; be they officers or a humble private such as George Trussell.

For once the initial attack was successful; the Canadians took Vimy Ridge. However, the Germans pushed reserves forward and the result of the battle of Arras which dragged on for over five weeks to 16th May was 150,000 British and 100,000 German casualties. Losses by the Canadians, Australians and other countries were huge.

Among these awful losses there is even some doubt as which day George was killed. One record shows that seventeen men in the 6th Battalion were killed on the 10th April, another that there were no reported casualties on the 10th but many on the 9th, the opening day of the offensive. In one sense, it matters little whether 9th or 10th. He was twenty-eight.

The body of Private George Trussell was never identified; at best he was buried in an unknown grave.

He is commemorated on the Arras

Near to Arras, Royal Engineers repairing a lock bridge to facilitate an advance.

Memorial, Pas de Calais, France, Bay 2. His name is engraved on one of the many panels.

This memorial commemorates almost 35,000 men from the UK, South Africa and New Zealand who died in the Arras sector between the spring of 1916 and August 1918, the eve of the *'Advance to Victory'*.

Private Trussell is on the Roll of Honour in the Regimental Chapel in Holy Trinity Church Guildford. The Book of Remembrance lists the 8000 men of The Queen's (Royal West Surrey) Regiment who gave their lives during the war.

The gap between the politics of the war and the soldiers' life is well shown in that George Trussell's death coincided with the United States of America's entry into the war. Both events were part of the Great War, yet seemingly far apart in every other respect. The politicians' or generals' decisions mattered little to George's mother Elizabeth. She had simply, but tragically, lost her son. Nothing is known of Elizabeth, after his death. There is no record of her being buried in Pirton; perhaps she moved away or remarried. She was only 31 when her husband died and 60 when her son was killed. Her son George was one of the huge numbers whom A J P Taylor referred to when he wrote of the later Battle of Arras: *'The only achievement of the battle of Arras was a fresh butcher's bill'*.

******

In Pirton, the sight of the Rev Erskine Langmore on his bicycle, satchel strapped to the crossbar, visiting an increasing number of his anxious and grieving parishioners as news came through from the Front, became an increasingly common sight. His beating of the patriotic drum and strict writings in the parish magazine may well have been influenced by his upbringing; his father had been a professional soldier. The Pirton Vicar had been born in a soldiers' camp in Punjab, and his father had shown great courage at the Siege of Lucknow in the Indian Mutiny, when his son was only a year old. Indeed, his father retired as Colonel Edward Ham Langmore, living until 1913. However, for all his patriotic fervour, the Rev. Erskine W Langmore showed himself to be a most caring man in the parish during the worst years of the war.

**Rev. Erskine Langmore
Vicar of Pirton 1903 - 1922**

Soldier 12: Monday 23rd April 1917

PRIVATE JOSEPH HANDSCOMBE

VILLAGE FAMILY LOSE SECOND SON

It is unlikely, amid the carnage around Arras, that news of the death of fellow villager George Trussell on 10th April had reached Private Joseph Handscombe before he, too, was killed - only a short distance away, thirteen days later. The initial onslaught, called the Second Battle of Arras, had begun on 9th April 1917, but the intense fighting continued into May. Joseph was killed on 23rd April, St. George's Day.

Joseph, like his older village mate George Trussell, had been a man with a simple lifestyle, growing up quietly in rural Pirton and then suddenly pitched into war and killed.

On 11th July 1916, Martha and George Handscombe had learnt of the death of their 22-year old son Frank. In the months following, they must have lived in dread for news of Joseph. Then nine months after the first death-blow, twenty year old Joseph was dead; their grief, too hard to imagine.

Joseph Handscombe was a true Pirton man; his ancestors were of the village and the family link continues to the present time. In 1883 George Handscombe, a 41 year old labourer, married 25-year old Martha Dawson, both of Pirton. A glance at the 1901 census confirms the size of the family and the local nature of the family's work, essentially dependent on the land. Ten children - whose ages spanned from twenty-two to one year old Hedley. Whilst some mechanisation had come into the parish, as shown by 59 year old George being employed as a farm engine driver, his children all followed traditional jobs. They were: a baker's assistant, a miller's carman delivering flour or seed, a farm labourer, a horse ploughboy and fifteen-year old Jane helping her mother at home with baby Hedley, as well as the four youngsters at the village school. A family which was typical of many in Pirton. Whilst humble village families like the Handscombes were hardworking, they were frequently denied full educational or economic advancement.

Joseph, born on 16th June 1896, was the ninth child. This large family lived in a thatched cottage *(as described in the earlier biography of Frank Handscombe).* Joseph's elder sister, Jane, was the mother of Margaret Ingram, and the late Joe Titmuss; both from Royal Oak Lane. Indeed, Joe was named after his uncle, Private Joseph Handscombe.

Joseph started school in 1899 and for the next ten years will have walked daily up the slight hill past both the old and new Methodist chapels, the centre of life for many of the Handscombes, to the village school. School was all about the 'three Rs' with large classes and rather unhygienic conditions. Most homes were crowded and water often had to be collected from a communal pump. It was not until the 1930s that mains water, sewage and electricity came to the village.

After leaving school, he worked on the land for

Whilst photographed a few years after the war, the Handscombe family home remained much the same.

An air of pre-war tranquillity seems to reign at Rectory Farm where Joseph first worked.

Mr E R Davis, who owned Rectory Farm. Like all the Handscombe family, he was very active in the Wesleyan Chapel and when his brother, Frank, joined up, Joseph took over as Sunday school leader. But it was not long before he enlisted at Ampthill, becoming Private Joseph Handscombe, 23086, of the 4th Battalion, Bedfordshire Regiment. A school contemporary, Sidney Baines, killed on the Somme in November 1916, had been in the same battalion.

In July 1916, Joseph heard the awful news that his brother, Frank, had been killed. By a terrible stroke of fate, Joseph landed in France on the very day his brother was killed. What Joseph's army service had been up until that day in July is not known. His journey to the Front was probably the same as for thousands of others: from an English training camp to the nearest station, train to Southampton, boat to Le Havre and brief stay in a rest camp. From the coast the men travelled by any available means, often railway for the first part and then horse drawn cart, taxi or even open-topped bus. Then would follow a march to a camp awaiting exact posting details, before finally reaching the Front

How much time Joseph was at the Front prior to April 1917 is unknown, although it is likely that he had experienced major action. Into April he was almost certainly caught up in the final preparations for the assault around Arras, just as George Trussell had been. The initial assault on Vimy Ridge and surrounds has been well chronicled and whilst Joseph survived that initial bloodbath, his death was not far away.

Extracts from the Battalion's war diary probably describes Joseph's final activities *(ORs = other ranks, namely not officers)*:

1-7 Apr 1917 - Manqueville Battalion in rest billets - Training.
8 Apr 1917 - Maisnil-les-Ruitz Battalion marched to MAISNIL LE RUITZ.
9-14 Apr 1917 Battalion standing by to move.
14 Apr 1917 - front line near Gavrelle Battalion moved to ARRAS by motor busses and took over line

Like all front line soldiers, Private Joseph Handscombe spent much of his war-life in trenches. Here a Lancashire Fusilier looks out on No Mans Land, the area between the trenches of the two sides.

from 23rd N.F.
15 Apr 1917 Reconnaissance of GAVRELLE in conjunction with 10/R.D.F.
Casualties Killed 2/Lts FREAR & MARSHALL WOUNDED left [Lieut?] WRAY 2/LTS. ROMAIN & MOGRIDGE. 55 O.Rs
16-21 Apr 1917 - support line near Arras Battalion relieved by 17/R.F.
22 Apr 1917 - front line facing Gavrelle Battalion moved to front line and occupied assembly trenches in front of GAVRELLE 189th Brigade on our right 17/R.F. on our left. Objective of Battalion - right boundary main road through GAVRELLE to the far side of the village. Left boundary GAVRELLE-OPPY system of trenches 200 yards North of GAVRELLE.
23 Apr 1917 *Attacked at 4.45 A.M.* captured village & reached objective. Shelled very heavily during the day and counter-attacked in the afternoon. Casualties - Killed 2/LT MULLIGAN 2/LT MUIR Wounded Capt BERRY 2/Lts PRIMROSE-WELLS, BRIDGES, LEWIS, Thomas, HUNT, KNAPP. *O.Rs. 260.* CAPT MILLS 2/LT Worth BRODIE, FISHWICK, MORRISH.

Among the 260 O.R. (other ranks) casualties on 23rd April, St. George's Day, were 68 dead. One of these was Private Joseph Handscombe, *'killed in action'*. He was a victim hauntingly prefaced by Shakespeare's immortal words of another battle, fought amid the mud some five centuries earlier. The Battle of Agincourt, fought only 35 miles away from Arras, had long been associated with St. George's Day and English courage ' *Once more unto the breach dear friends, once more; or close the wall up with our English dead.....*'

His was to become one of 35,000 names commemorated on the Arras Memorial (Bay 5), the same memorial that bears the name of George Trussell, who had died thirteen days earlier. Two other Pirton names were to be added later.

For Martha and George Handscombe, the news of the death of another son must have been appalling. When Armistice came the following year their grief continued; the mental scars of losing two sons were carried by them to their own resting places in St. Mary's churchyard.

Soldier 13: Died Tuesday 31st July 1917

CORPORAL HARRY SMITH

KILLED ON THE FIRST DAY OF PASSCHENDAELE

Family tragedies, unlike lightning, can strike in the same place more than once. For the Smith family, tragedy struck three times within eight months, both parents died and their son, Harry, was killed in Flanders.

Harry Smith was one of the 'Pirton Terriers'; men who had joined the Hertfordshire Territorials before the war started. These nine young men were filled with patriotic fervour; six of them were dead before the war was over.

Whilst little detail is known of Harry's wartime experiences they were undoubtedly horrendous.

He was traumatised by the shock of close comrades dying, before being killed at Passchendaele, the village that gave its name to the Third Battle of Ypres.

The Smith family was well-established in Pirton when, in 1869, James Smith a 20-year old labourer married Lydia Pearce. James, like most villagers at that time, was illiterate; signing with the oft-used 'X' mark when they were married at St. Mary's. However, the opening of the village school in 1877 made a huge difference to the generation of villagers later to fight in the Great War.

Harry, the youngest of Lydia and James' five children, was born on 15th August in the particularly hot summer of 1889. The family lived near to The Fox public house, in one of Holmes cottages, now part of 41 High Street. The parents had the most common Pirton occupations; James an agricultural worker, Lydia a straw-plaiter. Even before Harry and brother Frank went to the war, the family had suffered a tragedy when their brother, 29 year old John, died in 1911.

Harry worked on the land for Mr Franklin of Walnut Tree Farm before moving on to Spencers Engineering Works in Hitchin. With the Herts Territorials, he had already been to various training camps, including one at Berkhamsted.

The magnet of the war drew 25-year old Harry, along with some of his mates, and in August he became Private Harry Smith, 265408, 1st Battalion Hertfordshire Regiment. He was part of Company G, a tightly knit unit of local men; this comradeship was to carry them through both good times and appalling adversity. In a 1914 Christmas letter, he described conditions in the trenches: *'Very cold –first shave for 10 days. I have had one go at the Germans. There are four or five inches of snow'*.

By the autumn of 1915, he was Lance Corporal Harry Smith, the rank he held when best man to his great mate Arthur Walker at St. Mary's Pirton in November.

The close feelings between these men was never more heartbreakingly shown than when Harry was with his Pirton friends John Parsell, George Roberts and Arthur Walker, on the front line. In a barrage of German shells 18-year old Private John Parsell was killed and Arthur Walker fatally injured. Harry had been in the thick of battle for nearly two years; a short leave, in May 1916, being one of the few. He was so traumatised by John Parsell's death that he had to pass the wretched job of writing to John's parents to Private George Roberts. By the autumn of 1916, only two of the nine original Pirton 'Terriers' had not been wounded or killed.

Although details of Harry's war are sparse, letters home reveal how he and his mates made light of life at the Front. A letter, dated January 1917, from Private Sidney Smith, no relative but a member of the same unit, stated that he and his mates were all *'safe and sound'*. He described something of the condition of the trenches in which they often had to stand waist-deep in filthy water for twelve hours at a time, but wrote that they had good fires to go to afterwards, at which they dried their clothing!

He added:

'We started singing and the Germans heard us. They had the cheek to get on top of their trenches and waved their hats to us, but we soon made them get lower by putting a few bullets into them. They were only two hundred yards from us. We enjoyed ourselves on Christmas Day as well as we could expect, but live in hopes of having a better one next time. The Herts (regiment) have been lucky up to the present, and hope to remain lucky enough to get home safe, we are still merry and keep in good heart'.

A few weeks later, Harry wrote that a village friend at the Front was anxious that his sweetheart

'Should keep the rice handy for the wedding, as we shall soon be home to get married, when we will have a jolly good time - so cheer up, for we are not dead yet'.

Early in 1917, he was promoted to Corporal H Smith. On Tuesday 31st July, he set out on yet another dangerous operation, but was shot and killed just short of the objective. 2nd Lieutenant Aubrey Baker of the Herts regiment later wrote to Corporal Harry Smith's sister:

'He was seen to fall just before reaching our final objective. He was an excellent NCO and much loved by his section and the whole of the platoon. He will be greatly missed by us all. I can only offer you my deepest sympathy and hope that the cause for which he gave his life will help you to bear your sad loss'.

This was an early death in the horror of Passchendaele, the Third Battle of Ypres. Whereas the First and Second battles of Ypres were launched by the Germans, the Third Battle of Ypres was planned by the Allies with the intention of a major break through by Haig's forces in Flanders. Meticulously planned, the attack was launched on 31 July 1917, continuing until the fall of Passchendaele village on 6th November. However, Corporal Harry Smith was killed on the first day of the campaign. He was twenty-seven. On that day the first of many summer and autumn rains began to fall on Passchendaele.

He was buried in the largest of all war cemeteries, Tyne Cot, Zonnebeke, at West-Vlaanderen in Belgium, Ref, 10. D. 5. He is one of the five Pirton men on the Hertfordshire Territorials' Memorial at their Hitchin headquarters. Corporal Harry Smith had been born, went to school, grew up and worked in the quietness of rural North Hertfordshire. He died in the awfulness of countryside filled with shell-holes and filthy, stinking water so deep that horses and men were drowned; guns and even tanks disappeared in this ocean of slime.

Harry Smith died in a period of great family tragedy. Whilst in the trenches, he had learnt of the death of his father in December 1916 and less than four months later, that of his mother, pre-deceasing Harry by less than four months. His married sister Ruth and younger brother, Frank, received the fatal news. How much grief that family had to bear.

The lives of the 'Pirton Terriers' were being

shattered. John Parsell was the first of them to die, Arthur Walker the second and now Harry Smith. Later, three more were killed; only three of the original nine returned to Pirton.

A walk into the graveyard of St. Mary's, Pirton reveals a headstone (plot 1133) telling of this family tragedy. It records the deaths of parents James and Lydia Smith, of John (Harry's brother) in 1911, and at its foot the wording: *'Also of Harry Smith, killed in action July 31st 1917'*.

Harry's sister, Ruth, had married Harry Albert Cooper and they were the grandparents of Pete Lake now living in Walnut Tree Road – another village link with the past.

The headstone in St. Mary's churchyard tells the tragic story of the Smith family.

Soldier 14: Died Wednesday 1st August 1917

PRIVATE WILLIAM BAINES

SECOND PIRTON DEATH AT THE HORROR OF PASSCHENDAELE

'All villages had their extensive families and each of these families had a beginning.' Around 1815, young James Baines walked the dozen or so miles from his home near Ardeley in North Hertfordshire, espied the small settlement of Pirton and found casual work there. He could not have imagined that he was to become the patriarch of an extensive family, from which a century later at least nine men were to serve in the Great War; three to be killed. Two of these soldiers, Sidney and then William, were born and grew up in Pirton.

At the beginning of the twentieth century Pirton, like so many villages, had a complex network of families linked by a common ancestor; it was this family network that accentuated the grief when one of its members was killed in the war years. In 1901, the extended Baines family occupied eight cottages in the village with forty-four members.

James, patriarch of this family, was born in 1798 and living to the exceptional age of ninety-four, knew two of his many grandchildren who were later to die in the war. There was Sidney, who was killed on the Somme in November 1916. *(Soldier 8)*

Less than nine months later, Sidney's cousin, William who was 40 years old, was killed on another notorious battlefield, Passchendaele.

William's parents were Edwin and Annis Baines, living in one of the poor cottages round the main village green; he was the fourth of twelve children. Leaving school at thirteen, he was soon working in the nearby fields, but by the turn of the century he had moved on to be a domestic groom near Baldock, some nine miles away. He lodged there in Norton Street with Emma Smith, a widow, and her two teenage daughters, Mary and Emma. Mary and William fell in love and were married in the early part of 1902. Mary was a washerwoman.

William worked through a variety of jobs; a domestic worker at the time of his marriage to being a cab driver linked with a hotel, probably in Hitchin, some nine years later. Certainly by 1911, William and Mary were living at 17 Union Street in Hitchin. *(Near Chalkdell House, the old workhouse, off Oughtonhead Way).*

Just four miles away, the First Garden City of Letchworth was fast emerging. It may well have been the new housing in Letchworth that attracted the couple to move there; certainly they were living there by the time of William's enlistment in the war. No evidence has been found that they had any children.

By the outbreak of the war, William was thirty seven, older than many serving men. He enlisted as Private William Baines, service number 203741, the Bedfordshire

The first private house built in Letchworth Garden City. William Baines was one of the hundreds of men employed in building Letchworth at the beginning of the 20th century.

Regiment. Like many others, he may have joined up for feelings of patriotism or through social pressure, increasingly exerted on able-bodied men.

Changing regiments was not uncommon, particularly after recovering from wounds or an illness, and whilst initially with the Bedfords, he moved to the 12th Battalion of the East Surrey Regiment, no 204361. His battalion became part of the 122nd Brigade in the 41st Division in X Corps of the 2nd Army.

We cannot be sure of William's war-time movements, but we can follow his most likely path. On the 31st July 1917, the 41st Division was some three miles south east of Ypres, about to enter the Third Ypres campaign. Overhead air battles raged, as British and French air forces sought to destroy German observation balloons and planes, making the German gunners' task harder. The rain had already begun to fall as zero hour approached. This was to be at 3.50am when the 122nd Brigade attacked south of the Ypres-Comines Canal. The East Surreys, William's battalion, were in support. By the end of the day the brigade had consolidated itself in the ruins of the village of Hollebeke, only 100 yards short of its objective. The East Surreys then came up and pushed on to capture a farm just south west of Hollebeke.

The advance on this fateful day was on an eleven mile front, but the already appalling conditions worsened. In the previous week, 3,000 guns had hurled almost five tons of shells at every yard of the front. This preliminary bombardment had damaged the water table and the rain could not run away. The whole area was a particularly foul one with the mud defying belief, many men found themselves up to armpits in this quagmire and when comrades tried to pull them out they, too, might well have been sucked in. Entire

Private William Baines is commemorated at The Menin Gate Memorial to the Missing at Ypres. The Memorial carries the names of 56,000 soldiers of the British Empire who fell in the Ypres Salient before 15th August 1917 and have no known grave.

platoons were overwhelmed in bogs as treacherous as any quicksand. If feet strayed from the maze of duck-boards, drowning was a potential outcome; now even the duckboards were bombarded and sinking. Floods of rain and a blanket of mist saturated and cloaked the whole of this seemingly desolate Flanders plain. Like some engulfing monster the shell holes filled with water and the mud became an ever deepening morass, stinking and foul with the decay of rotting horses and men. Any chance of exploiting the initial success was destroyed by the continuing dreadful weather. All through the night of that last day in July it rained steadily, and for four days afterwards.

The casualties were enormous. General Sir Douglas Haig, the C-in-C, had been advised not to order the advance but, encouraged by previous though slight success, he disregarded this advice. It was this battle that earned him the name of 'The Butcher'. On 31st July or Wednesday 1st August all trace of William disappeared. How he was killed will never be known. No burial spot, no body was ever identified. He was 40, one of the two oldest Pirton men to die.

He is commemorated on Panel 34 of the Menin Gate Memorial at Ypres along with the other 55,000 men who were lost without trace in the Ypres Salient. Additional to the Pirton War Memorial, he is also remembered on the Memorial in Letchworth, his adopted town.

Within twenty-four hours, Pirton had lost two men, both killed within a few miles of each other, both victims of Passchendaele. Corporal Harry Smith was killed on that first day of Passchendaele, now Private William Baines on the second day.

Mary, his wife, mourned, almost certainly seeking solace with her mother and sister.

Although his home had been in Letchworth, William was a Pirton man and it was there that news of his death spread like wildfire through the many lines of the Baines family, to neighbours, to his former mates – at least those who were still around. But while his death became known, the full horrors of the trenches, the mud, the wastelands, the canons, machine-guns and barbed wire only emerged later.

****

As the women in the village of Pirton walked to Frank Andrews shop in downtown Pirton or to have their children's shoes repaired in John Thrussell's shop, they spoke in sombre tones.

'Did you know that Annis' boy was killed? That's another poor lad from the village that's dead. Surely, there won't be any more; surely the war will soon be over.'

These were certainly their thoughts and if these words were spoken, the answers were to prove far worse over the next fifteen months. Villagers became ever more anxious as neighbours lost husbands, sons, brothers and loved ones. The sense of loss could be found in every house, seen in every face. Yet it was to become worse.

This very faded picture taken around 1910, shows neighbours chatting by Great Green. Three of the ladies in the group were soon to lose sons in the war, including Annis Baines *(third from left)* **the mother of Private William Baines.**

Soldier 15: Died Tuesday 9th October 1917

LANCE CORPORAL WILLIAM THOMAS HILL

LOVE FOR A PIRTON LASS BROUGHT HIM TO THE VILLAGE

Of the 30 names on the War Memorial, William (Tommy) Hill is one of only two who appears not to have lived in the village. His first visit to Pirton was to meet his fiancé's family.

This is a story of these two young people; he a Gloucestershire man, she a village lass from Pirton. They met at an Earl's castle, were united in love, married and looked forward to a life together. They were then separated by the war and, tragically, all their hopes were snatched away by the young husband's death; another Passchendaele fatality. To add to her agony, his widow, Florence, was uncertain of his death for more than a year.

William's story

The Hill family were Gloucestershire people, but as a railway worker James Hill had to move home. It was whilst in Bodelwyddan in north-east Wales that his wife Annie Eliza gave birth, in 1888, to their first child, William Thomas Hill. However, by the time William was three years old, the family had settled back in Gloucestershire and were living at number 1 Ivy Cottage in Pembroke Road, Shirehampton, some five miles from Bristol. It seems likely that he was known by his family as William; only later that he was called Tommy, his second name. His grandparents, Nancy and William Hill, were living at 2 Avon View Cottage, in the same road as young William and his parents.

By the turn of the century, still at Ivy Cottage, William had two brothers, James and Clement and two sisters, Nancy and Elesia. Sometime later the family moved to 2 Avonview Cottage where William's grandparents had lived after running the 'Rising Sun', a local public house.

Leaving school in 1900, William worked as a gardener in Shirehampton. It was through his acquired skills that he later moved seventy miles to work in the extensive grounds of Highclere Castle south of Newbury, the magnificent home of the 5th Earl of Carnarvon. By 1911, the 25 year old William was sharing simple accommodation

Highclere Castle

provided by the owners of Highclere at the Bothy, part of the great house.

Florence's story

The Carter family were Hertfordshire people. Charles Carter was born in Bengeo and became a police constable in his 20s. His duties caused him to move to a succession of small villages and whilst stationed at Buckland, near Barkway in North Hertfordshire, he met a local girl whom he married.

The years passed and after a spell at Datchworth, Charles and his wife Eliza moved on to Pirton, where they lived in the police house, part of Middle Farm off Crabtree Lane. By 1891 the Carters had become a large family with eleven of their children living at home: Elizabeth was 20, Henry 19, George 17, Alice 14, Ellen 12, Ernest 11, Annie 8, Walter 6, Daisy 5, Florence 4, and Ester Kate 2. The eldest, Charles, age 21, was living away and Arthur had died in 1890 age 14.

It is on Florence Rachael, born on 16th July 1886, that attention is focused. The younger members of the family attended the village school, which had opened in 1877. Florence would have worked and played alongside Fred Burton, Albert Abbiss, George Trussell and others who were later killed in the 1914-18 War.

By 1901 her father, Charles, had retired as village policeman, becoming one of the pillars of this rural community as a local overseer, collecting rates from the landowners to administer to the many needy people in this poor village. He was also an important figure in St. Mary's church. Charles and Eliza now lived in one of the cottages (now called Ashburn) on the west side of Burge End Lane.

St. Mary's Church, a central part of life in this quiet village, played an important part in Florence's life, too. For her endeavours, she won a Bible, now a proud possession of Joan Burton who provided much help with the couple's story. Florence's younger sister, Kate, married Frank Burton and their son married Joan.

When she won her Bible, Florence was a mothers' help, caring for young village children. By 1911, she had become one of ten servants working at the substantial Broxbournebury mansion in East Hertfordshire. This property, owned by George Smith Bosanquet, had been in that family for over a century. A while later, she took a job in an even more impressive residence; this was to prove life-changing. Her service skills took her to work at Highclere Castle in Hampshire.

Love, Marriage and Grief

Thus, Tommy (as she always called him) and Florence found themselves as two of the large workforce in this 19th century 'castle'. It was there that they met and fell in love. Tommy was a gardener in the grounds which had been designed by Capability Brown. Florence a relatively lowly domestic, working in this home of the Earl of Carnarvon whose passion was for the lost civilisation of Ancient Egypt. He later sponsored Howard Carter, who discovered the astonishing treasure of the tomb of Tutankhamun in the Valley of the Kings, the richest burial site ever found.

It is not known how often Tommy and Florence managed to visit Pirton, but on 16th September 1914 they were married at St. Mary's, the village church. The only sadness was that Florence's father, Charles, had died two months previously.

It is not known where the couple first lived, but the address given in 1918 was Commercial Road in Peckham, south-east London. In

Some members of the Carter family outside their house in Burge End Lane. Florence is wearing the flamboyant hat.

the latter part of 1916, Tommy enlisted in Marlborough; perhaps they were still living at Highclere or were on route to see his parents. He was sent to the 4th Training and Draft Finding Battalion stationed at Barry Docks in South Wales. After basic training he was transferred in February 1917 to the 2nd/8th Lancashire Fusiliers, service no. 307763 and with his unit moved to Colchester, as preparations were made to go to France.

Boarding a train to Southampton, the overcrowded boat took the men to Le Havre and on by train to Thiennes. For months they served around Givenchy, later at Arques near St. Omer. Then came the move to the major battle area on the Ypres-Menin Road and, on 9th October, Tommy and his regiment were engaged in the joint operation with Australian troops in the Battle of Poelcapelle. Lance Corporal Tommy Hill was one of thousands killed in this area, to become forever called Passchendaele. The exact place of his death was never known, his body like so many men, never found. He was 29.

That his body was never identified began an agony of waiting for Florence, his parents and loved ones. They did not know what had happened to him and ten months after his death, the Pirton Vicar wrote that he was still 'missing'. We cannot tell when Florence's hopes of Tommy being found alive ended, but thoughts of him being a prisoner or being injured in France, remained until after the war was over. As for so many other women, not knowing, must have been almost unbearable. She would also have been concerned about her brothers, Ernest and Walter Edward who were also serving abroad.

For James and Eliza, Tommy's parents, waiting through this period of dreadful uncertainty, there was a second tragedy. Their youngest son, James, was killed on 31st March 1918.

Tommy is commemorated on the Tyne Cot Memorial, Panel 55; his name inscribed on the War Memorial of Shirehampton, his home town, and Pirton, his loving wife's home village. Corporal Harry Smith from Pirton is also commemorated at Tyne Cot.

Her husband's death occurred just three years into their marriage; much of that time spent apart during those war years. She never remarried and soon moved from south-east London to Bunyan Road in Hitchin, to be near her family. She was especially close to her youngest sister Kate who then lived in Burge End Farm in Pirton, to which Florence was a frequent visitor. She died around 1950, a widow for over 30 years.

Kate's son was given the name Thomas, in memory of her favourite sister's husband.

The name of Lance Corporal 'Tommy' Hill is also on the War Memorial in Shirehampton, the Gloucestershire village where he grew up.

Soldier 16: Died Tuesday 23rd October 1917

CORPORAL ALBERT TITMUSS

'THOU LEAVEST ME TO GRIEVE' – HIS WIDOW MOURNS FOR 53 YEARS

Each Pirton war-death, each sacrifice was individually traumatic, but perhaps too little thought is given to their loved ones who were left to grieve – wives, sweethearts, parents, sisters and brothers, extended family and friends. The tragedy for the grieving ones, whose lives were blighted, sometimes destroyed, is nowhere clearer than with the death of Corporal Albert John Titmuss. He died in 1917 aged 33; his widow bore her grief for 53 years.

Albert, born on 18th June 1884, was one of George and Emma Titmuss's eight children; three sons and five daughters. When Albert started at the village school the family lived in The Baulk, off Shillington Road; only a stone's throw from where the original, timber-constructed village Methodist Chapel had stood. Another poor family, George was often away wherever seasonal work could be found; Emma earning a few pence as one of over 250 strawplaiters in the village.

At the turn of the century Albert, working on one of the local farms, lived with his parents and four of his siblings. His younger brother Freddie later became a professional footballer, playing for Southampton and England in the 1920s.

Emma, his mother, died in 1909. Two years later, Albert still lived at home along with his father, sister Lillian and two brothers, Sidney and Freddie. However, it was not long before his father moved to Church Walk, part of the later demolished Middle Farm off Crabtree Lane. By this time, Albert was probably lodging during the week with other Pirton railwaymen near Finsbury Park. It was there he worked for the Great Northern Railway (amalgamated to become the LNER in 1923). For some years he had known his future wife, Elsie Goldsmith from Pirton; indeed Elsie's father, Fred, also worked at Finsbury Park.

On 16th August 1915, Albert a strongly built 31 year-old in the prime of life, enlisted with the Royal Field Artillery, "B Battery, 169th Brigade, service number L/37084. Seven months later, when he and Elsie married at St Mary's on 20th March 1916, there began that all too frequent tragedy of a promised family life cut short by the tragedy of war. Elsie was 23; one of eight children living in a small two-up and two-down cottage, at what is now an extended no. 5 Walnut Tree Road, the home of Janet Brown. This house has been with the same family for over a century, as Janet's mother, Effie, was the sister of Albert's wife.

Albert and Elsie had no time to make a family home, forced to delay that until the war was over. With war deaths soaring, Albert left England for France in May 1916, less than two months after their marriage. Elsie and Albert wrote frequently to each other, but their first wedding anniversary passed with them having shared so little married life together.

His father, George, died of a stroke whilst working on Mr Brown's farm at Welbury in November 1916, but Albert was unable to attend the funeral due to front-line duties. He did manage to get home on a short leave in mid-December.

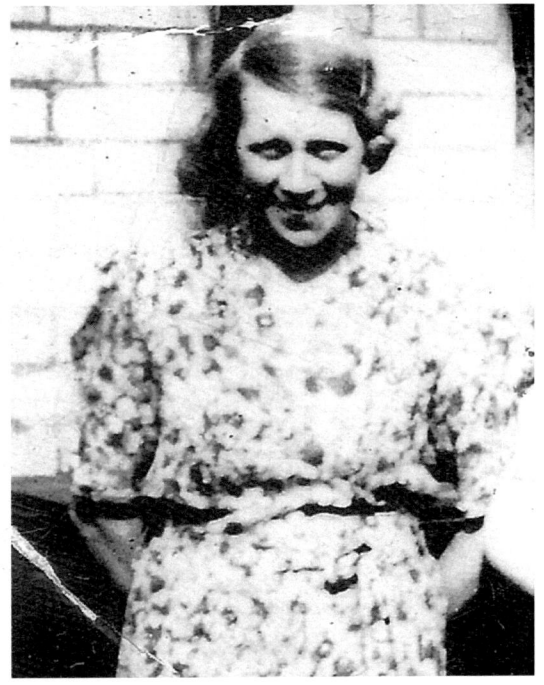

Young Elsie Titmuss

In September 1917, he was back on leave with his beloved young wife. Whilst his return to the village must have been bliss for them, the countdown of days for his return to the trenches must have been unbelievably distressing. Did Elsie know George Eliot's words: *'In every parting, there is an image of death'*? Tragically, when he returned to France on 7th October, he had seen his young wife for the last time. Two weeks later he was dead, Elsie a widow.

This reliable and popular corporal was almost certainly manning the howitzers in the fury of Passchendaele (Third Battle of Ypres), which had already claimed the lives of two of his Pirton mates, Harry Smith and William Baines. The noise of battle, not least of the howitzers, would have been horrendous. Another member of the Royal Field Artillery wrote:

'It was mud, mud, everywhere: mud in the trenches, mud in front of the trenches, mud behind the trenches. Every shell-hole was a sea of filthy oozing mud. I suppose there's a limit to everything, but the mud of Passchendaele – to see men sinking in to the slime, dying in the slime – I think it absolutely finished me off.'

On 23rd October, Albert, along with his mates in his battery, was preparing guns for action when a German shell exploded nearby. Colleagues got the terribly injured Albert to a place of safety and a doctor dressed his wounds, but he died before reaching the dressing station.

Corporal Albert Titmuss was buried at the Perth (China Wall) Cemetery (Ref VI.J.7), named after a major communications trench known as the Great Wall of China. This is near the village of Zillebeke in Flanders, a mile or so from the village of Ypres. The British took over the cemetery in June 1917 and after the Armistice it was greatly enlarged with more than 2,500 reburials from twenty-eight smaller cemeteries.

Although war deaths were becoming common in the village, the loss of her beloved Albert caused grief to Elsie of unremitting intensity. A young wife receiving the news that she had dreaded; the end to dreams of a life together. She received a thoughtful letter from Sergeant Gay, in whose battery her husband had been; how much comfort it brought to Elsie one cannot know. Having told her how her husband had died he wrote:

"His last thoughts were of you. He gave me your address and I promised him I would write. Please accept deepest sympathies from myself and comrades who respected him as a brave and fearless man... a true and honest comrade, respected by all NCOs and men in the battery'.

Albert Titmuss' war and life were over, but his widow's grief was to last a further 53 years. Janet, now living in the family home, recalls how her mother, Elsie's sister, told her of Elsie's inconsolable distress. *'She seemed to turn white overnight and would not leave her room for days;*

meals taken to her, remained mainly uneaten.'

The family tried everything to help Elsie overcome the misery, encouraging her to help choose the names of her brothers' and sisters' children. It was her choice that her niece, Janet, was so baptised. In 1941 Elsie's mother died, her father five years later. Elsie then lived on alone in the house where she had received the news of her husband's death over two decades previously. She never remarried and so brief was her marriage, that she was still known by some of her friends as Elsie Goldsmith.

But whilst not having the life of which she must have dreamed, Elsie became a tireless worker for St. Mary's Church and did much for the community; a Sunday School teacher and friend to all. She played the major part in raising money for the present blue carpet that runs down the aisle at St. Mary's Church. Elsie died in 1969, aged 76. To ensure the house in Walnut Tree Road stayed in the family, it was purchased by Janet and Bill Brown and Janet still lives there; the house in which the tragic news had reached her aunt over 90 years ago.

On Elsie's death, the Rev. Canon Arthur Suffrin wrote a lovely and telling epitaph, including the words:

'The death of Mrs Elsie Titmuss removes from our sight a faithful worshipper and worker in church and village. She was a widow for half a century, and kept flowers on the war memorial window throughout the year in memory of her husband and other Pirton men who lost their lives in war.'

In St. Mary's Garden of Rest, there is a stone marking where the ashes of Elsie Titmuss were placed. As Pirton men's names were inscribed on the War Memorial, it was left to their war widows, sweethearts, parents and family to grieve.

Elsie Titmuss *(on the left)* **gave a lifetime of service to St. Mary's and the community.**

'Thou leavest me to grieve', part of the subtitle of this writing, is from 'To Wordsworth,' by Percy Bysshe Shelley

Soldier 17: Died Sunday 2nd December 1917

SERGEANT FRED BURTON

CAMBRIDGE SERVANT, BERKSHIRE BUTLER AND SOLDIER

By the autumn of 1917, the massed armies were exhausted in the sea of mud and futility that made up the Western Front. The situation for Britain was mixed; USA had finally sent troops into the war, but Italy had collapsed and the Russians were on the verge of cutting a deal with the Germans. Politicians and generals blundered on and Britain's supremo, Field Marshal Haig, sent his Chief-of Staff to the fighting zone for the first time. As his car struggled through the mud, he burst into tears and cried: *'Good God, did we really send men to fight in that?' 'It's worse further up'*, replied his companion.

Further up, the British soldiers were beyond tears. Somewhere in the midst of these thousands of soldiers was a scattering of Pirton men, among them brothers, Fred and Sydney Burton. Sometime in the fateful year of 1917, the brothers had met at the Front and embraced. Sydney, four years older, came home on a short leave and told his mother that Fred was safe and looked forward to his return to England. That was not to be; on Sunday 2nd December 1917 Fred was killed.

His parents, David and Rose, had married in the 1870's; their romance kindled when Rose Walker's family owned the Shoulder of Mutton pub in Hambridge Way (burnt down in 1928). David Burton belonged to another well-represented village family of which Goliath, who lived in Crabtree House, was probably the best known. David and Rose took over another pub, the Red Lion, raising four children of whom Fred was the youngest; born on 29th January 1888.

By the turn of the century, the family's economic state had improved and they moved to a smallholding at Great Green. In that corner of the village green was a sizeable piece of land (now embracing no. 16) stretching back to the present Priors Hill. They also took on a plot of ten acres at the other end of the village, off Holwell Road,

as well as renting further acres within the parish. But whilst the family's fortune thrived, Fred decided to try his luck elsewhere.

Fred's career took him to residences very different to anything in Pirton. 1901 found him as a lowly servant in a most unlikely setting. Quite how this 13-year old got into service to a 75 year-old Cambridge University academic is unknown; maybe through some village connection. The academic was Professor Edward Byles Cowell, a translator of Persian poetry and the first Professor of Sanskrit at Cambridge University. Young Fred worked in the same household as the Professor, his two nieces and middle aged servants. His position came to an end when his elderly employer died in 1903.

Fred moved to Berkshire where he worked for Mr Lestocq Robert Erskine at Binfield Manor, near Bracknell. This widowed financier shared the large mansion with his daughter Muriel who was married to Sandford William Luard of a London Livery Company, three granddaughters and a grandson. To satisfy this large household there

Binfield Manor, Berkshire - in 1866

were eleven servants, one of whom was the butler, Fred Burton. Fred's work at Binfield Manor was a step up the ladder, a job which allowed little time for his interests of playing cricket and, occasionally, the violin. However, career prospects ended abruptly with the outbreak of war.

Fred travelled the few miles to Reading where he enlisted with the Princess Charlotte of Wales Royal Berkshire Regiment. Fred, a stocky and jovial-looking man, was among its first soldiers. He was twenty-six, competent at his work and he gained promotion. The next three years took him to many fighting points on the Western Front and by 1917 he was Sergeant Burton, 200950, 2nd/4th Battalion of the Berkshires. In February 1917, he had a brief leave and visited his mother, who was poorly, at her Great Green farmhouse.

His regiment was one of many to be engaged in the battle for Cambrai, an important railhead held by the Germans. The allies' attack was launched at dawn on 20th November 1917 with well over 400 tanks accompanied by six infantry and two cavalry divisions, plus a further 1,000 guns. In order to keep the attack a surprise, it was not preceded by the normal artillery bombardment. There was considerable initial success.

Fred was but one of the thousands of allied troops in the ferocious fighting, which in the end gained little ground, but claimed many lives. As the British used up their strength, the Germans counter-attacked on 30th November. The initial speed of the German infantry's advance was completely unexpected by the British and in the midst of the ensuing fighting, on Sunday 2nd December, Sergeant Fred Burton was killed. Between 20th November and 8th December, allied casualties were 44,207, of whom some 15,000 were killed and over 6,000 British soldiers taken prisoner

In Pirton, his mother's health worsened and she became desperately worried that there was no word from Fred. She contacted her son's former place of work, Binfield Manor, where Mrs Muriel

Luard had taken over ownership following the death of her father in 1916. Mrs Luard got in touch with the authorities and, with a heavy heart, informed Mrs Burton on 14th December that Fred had been killed twelve days earlier. He was 29. Another death, another letter of sympathy to be written, another family to grieve.

The initial gain in the battle was accompanied by church bells ringing in Britain, though not in Pirton although the bells had sounded two months previously, *'To celebrate recent successes in Belgium and Mesopotamia'*. All were premature peals, for it soon became obvious that this First Battle of Cambrai was a failed operation and on the day after Fred's death, Haig ordered an abandonment of virtually all the territory gained. Stories began to filter back of headlong retreat; of Generals caught in their pyjamas, and of new, German tactics that sliced through the British defences. Rumour and truth merge in time of war.

Whilst Fred had been away from the village for some years, he was well remembered by many in Pirton. For the second successive Christmas, the village was stunned by news of further war deaths, this time of Fred Burton and Walter Reynolds on the same day.

His brothers, Sydney and Thomas decided that Fred be remembered and a memorial card was made. This card was passed down within the family and still survives. Thomas was the father of Audrey Ford, who died in 2008, and she treasured the card dedicated to her uncle. Fred's brothers and his sister Beatrice had a headstone erected in St. Mary's churchyard which reads:

'Husband & father David Burton died 28 Feb 1916 age 58, also wife Rose Fanny died 22 Dec 1917 aged 58, also their son Sgt Fred Burton 2/4 Royal Berks Rgt killed in France 2 December 1917, age 29.'

Fred was buried in Fifteen Ravine British Cemetery, Villers-Plouich, Nord, France, Ref VIII D 17. The cemetery's name was derived from a ravine which was once bordered by fifteen trees. Over 1200 men are buried there, many brought from other graves after the armistice.

One final family memory was that Fred had owned a violin which was subsequently passed on to a family friend, Phil Abbiss, who also lived on Great Green.

Fred, later described by the family as dying in the *'Great battle of Cambrai'*, was killed on the same day as another Pirton victim, Walter Reynolds. They were the last two Pirton men to die in 1917, but thirteen more were soon to lose their lives.

Fred's father had died twenty months previously. It may have been a coincidence, but Fred's mother died on 22nd December 1917, just a week after she learnt of his death. She was only 58.

The treasured family memorial card to Sergeant Fred Burton.

Soldier 18: Died Sunday 2nd December 1917

PRIVATE WALTER REYNOLDS

OF SIX SOLDIER SONS, ONE GASSED AND NOW ONE KILLED

The emerging signs of wealth that reached into the cities by late Victorian times had failed to touch rural villages, like Pirton. The families were, in the main, poor and, above all, large. From a later perspective, it seems improbable that the small cottages with their simple two up and two down rooms housed families of eight, ten or even more. It was not unusual for some of the older children to set out in the evening with a bedroll to sleep at a cousin's or neighbour's home, where there was a little more sleeping space.

The Reynolds family was one such large family who, by 1886, lived at no. 3 Wesley Cottages, a small dwelling behind Cromwell Terrace, where the Village Stores now thrives. Head of the household was Lewis Reynolds, a chimney sweep known by all for the donkey and cart carrying his brushes. His wife Mary Ann (nee Catterell) from nearby Stondon was another villager who earned a meagre amount through straw plaiting, the product later taken to Hitchin en route for the hat and allied industry in Luton.

The common village pattern of small cottage, large family and low income was the Reynolds' lot. When first married they had lived in New Road, one of the Holwell Road cottages. Mary bore fifteen children; the first two, James and Clara, dying in their early years. Then Maria was born in 1874, Jacob 1876, Peggy 1877, Daisy 1880, Mary 1881, William 1884, Albert 1884, Abigail 1886; Sarah 1888, twins George and Harry in 1890, Emily 1893 and finally Walter in 1894.

The children went to the village school before seeking a job, usually in the village or in its surrounding land. They shared the hardships and joys of a large and close family. Their Uncle Jack, Aunt Ann and family lived next door. Life was not easy, but all seemed well in the first decade of the 20th century.

In addition to being the local sweep, Lewis had a small plot of land off Holwell Road. On leaving school, Walter helped his father on that smallholding and was later described as having, *'A fine, upright character, his considerateness and kindliness being a comfort to those dear to him'*.

By 1911, young Walter seems to have been the only one of the children still living at home. Like some of his village mates, the strong-jawed Walter had joined the Hitchin Territorials in March 1914. Five months later, came the hammer blow of the Great War. For Walter it was a small step to enlist in the village as Private 242137 in

The picture from a local newspaper, accompanying news of the death of Private Walter Revnolds.

the Hertfordshire Regiment, later transferred to 2nd/5th Battalion Gloucestershire Regiment.

The war raged, then stagnated in the trenches of Western Europe, producing terrible numbers of wounded and dead. It just happened that the six Reynolds boys were of a certain age, living at the wrong time; young men whom this war of madness enveloped.

Whatever the sons felt, the newspapers recorded their courage and bravery. *'Few families have a better record of war service than the Reynolds Family'* a local journalist, far from the Front, wrote. But their parents must have lived each day in great fear for their six sons. Walter from the Herts Regiment but attached to the Gloucester Regiment, William in the King's Shropshire Light Infantry in France, Driver Albert Royal Garrison Artillery, Driver Harry with the Royal Horse Artillery, already badly gassed in France, George in the Suffolk Regiment and Jacob serving on the home front. Two of the six sons, Walter and Albert were both killed in the last eleven months of the war.

To their parents in Pirton, each day, each week must have seemed an eternity for very little news filtered through. The generals spoke of victories, to the men and their families there was no victory - just anguish. Some of the Reynolds' boys had married and set up homes away from the village, but now it was a family in peril. Between them, the sons had (at least) twelve children.

On 24th May 1916, Walter was posted to France, spending most of the next nineteen months in the front line. In October 1917, he came home on leave, a brief period of sanity; leave intended every twelve months for other ranks had now become closer to every eighteen months. One can imagine him proudly arriving in uniform, feted by his parents and those of his siblings and friends still in the village. Home to the cottage just off the High Street, walking down and casting an eye over his father's plot in Holwell Road. On 28th October, his leave finished and he returned to the appalling conditions of war.

It seems that he went to the Front near Cambrai. This was the scene of repeated fighting and from 20th November of a huge battle. The exact circumstances of his death are uncertain, but we know that whilst he was resting on his way back to the Front, a nearby ammunition dump exploded. Walter's death was described as 'instant'. He was 23. The date of his death was 2nd December 1917, although recorded in some newspapers as 1st or 3rd December.

Less than two months after seeing their son, Lewis and Mary's joy turned to grief; another telegram arriving in the village. This was soon followed by a letter from Rev J Panton explaining the awfulness of the explosion that had caused

Marching to the Front

their son's death; no further detail as to the cause of the explosion but, perhaps, the detail did not matter to Lewis and Mary Reynolds. Their youngest son, just 23, was dead. Christmas Day 1917 must have been enveloped not in joy, but sadness, for it was on that very morning that the official report of Walter's death reached them.

They must have read the Revd. Panton's letter with unbelievably heavy hearts:

'I read the burial service over the spot where he and others were killed and their remains interred. I want to say how deeply his loss is regretted by all who knew him. He attended my services constantly and we have worshipped together in many strange places. May our Heavenly Father comfort you.'

His commanding officer, CF Hamilton added:

'These men are so splendid and you have every reason to be proud of them, but it is hardest of all for you at home, as, the men themselves say "You must try and keep a brave heart as he would wish and a bright hope for the future."'

Private Walter Reynolds is commemorated on the Cambrai Memorial, Louverval (Panel 6). He is one of five Pirton men on the Hertfordshire Territorials' Memorial in Hitchin.

Eight months later, the family tragedy was repeated when another of their sons, Albert, was killed. Another Pirton family had been ripped apart through the war. Mary had long been an invalid in the family home; now her heart, too, was forever shattered. Aubrey Reynolds who lives in the village can well remember visiting her at her home and recounts how she spent many years as an invalid in bed.

Throughout 1918, subscriptions towards a 'War Memorial Shrine' were shown in the parish magazine. Lewis and Mary subscribed in April; little realising that another one of their sons would be added eight months later.

Private Walter Reynolds is commemorated on the Cambrai Memorial.

Soldier 19: Died Tuesday 26th February 1918

LANCE CORPORAL ARTHUR ODELL

OLD VILLAGE FAMILY SUFFERS A TERRIBLE LOSS

The Odell family lost two sons in the war; the first, 21 years-old Arthur. The Odells were one of the longest established families in the village; as the roots of the family ran deep and wide, so did the grief at Arthur's death.

A century and a half earlier, Richard Odell had registered as a member of the local militia established to counter the threat of invasion from France. He was not called to serve and continued at his smithy near the village pond. Five generations later, his descendent Arthur Odell joined the militia to withstand the threat of the Kaiser's Germany; he served for three and a half years, dying before his twenty-second birthday.

It may be fanciful to suggest that the first Odell in Pirton goes back to Anglo Saxon times, when someone bearing that name left the small village in North Bedfordshire called Odell. Descendants from that lineage spread to surrounding counties with a variety of derivatives, such as: O'Dell, Odel, Odal, Odele Odle, Odal.

It was from John Odell and Mary (nee Dawson) that a new generation was born: Jane (in 1881) followed by James (1883), Martha (1885), Robert (1886), Nellie (1888), Frank (1890), William (1894) Arthur (4th May 1896), John (1898, who died in infancy), Frederick (1899) and Margerie (1902). Arthur, eighth in this line of a large Pirton family, is the one on whom we concentrate.

The family had lived in one of the Holwell Road cottages and later in Silver Street or, as shown on the 1911 census, Dead Horse Lane. More recently it was renamed with the grander title of Royal Oak Lane. They lived at number 2, to become no. 12; an attractive house now, then a small, thatched cottage.

Arthur would have walked each day to school, past the village pond, the four or five small shops in the main village road, 'The Fox' and 'Live and

Let Live' public houses. As with many of the village families, church or chapel played an important part. The Odells were adherents to St. Mary's Church; indeed Arthur gained prizes for his regular attendance at the Sunday school and a prize for his knowledge of the church catechism.

It is not known which men were helped by their Christian faith. However, unsigned letters from 'The Front' in the Parish Magazine often mentioned the support from their faith. Through his upbringing, Arthur Odell may have been one such man.

His school days were mainly under the stern eye of the new headmaster, Mr Arthur Donson and the education was sound. Arthur left school in 1908 and for at least three years worked as a farm labourer. Some time later he worked for a patent yeast firm, Bishof & Brooke of 24 Bucklersbury

The Odell family lived for a time in one of these cottages in Holwell Road, a terrace where other families, too, lost a son in the war. It was a row of cottages known variously as 'The 12 Apostles' and 'Merry Arse Row'. The latter suggesting that some of the poorer children wore nothing to cover their backsides!

in Hitchin. He spent most of the day taking the yeast to a variety of the town's bakeries.

The clouds of war were fast darkening and certainly Arthur and his village friends talked endlessly about the opportunities of joining up. Early in 1914, Arthur, still only 17, enlisted as a Territorial with the 1st Hertfordshire Regiment, one of the first of nine Pirton lads to do so. Later, in a local paper, he was described as one making up 'Pirton's *Sacrifice*', although the ultimate sacrifice was to be delayed until he was 21.

He was in France during the first month of the war and in late 1914, even though away from the front line for a brief period. He wrote:

'(We) can hear the guns....and want to get up there again. The French relieved us first time we went in the trenches. All the Pirton lads in 1st Herts are quite well and happy'.

Christmas Eve and Christmas Day were spent digging trenches and there the men stayed until 20th January.

His baptism by fire had started early, and it was not long before he received a bullet wound to his arm, which the local newspaper described as a *'noble scar of battle'*. In June 1915 he was again wounded, this time having to return to England. He was sent to Norwich hospital where, even after two operations, there was still a bullet in his arm. However, it was not long before he was back in the front-line.

Through a letter from Private Goldsmith, another Pirton soldier, we know that early in 1916, Arthur met up with John Parsell and Fred Baines. Growing up together, attending the same school and all joining up in the early months of the war caused a close bond between these young men. In one of the most wretched periods of the Great War, Arthur and his two mates shared a brief memory of village days with talk of loved ones back in Pirton, reminiscences of village people and teenage haunts which must have seemed so far from those awful trenches. In just over two years, all three were united in death, their names forever linked on the Village War Memorial.

By the time of their reunion in 1916, the war had taken such a terrible toll on lives, that regiments were being reorganised. Arthur, along with other Hertfordshire Regiment men, moved to the transport section of the 13th Battalion of the Royal Sussex Regiment, service number G15640. He was wounded again, this time in the leg, but not before being promoted to lance-corporal. He was to see the village once more, on a short leave in November 1917, a brief reunion with his parents and family. There would have been few of his old Pirton schoolmates to share a drink with at a local pub – they were away, fighting their own battles.

On 26th February 1918, an event stunned the country when German torpedoes sunk the Glenart Castle, a clearly marked hospital ship in the English Channel; 186 people died. On that same day, almost unnoticed, Arthur Odell was killed in action, fighting somewhere near Cambrai.

The news of his death was another shattering blow to the villagers. Deaths of Pirton men were running at one each month; a frequency almost unbearable to imagine in such a small village. The telegram arrived; the grief of the family began – increasing a terrible communal grief and anxiety in the village. Little solace can have been gained by the letter from Sgt J Watt, who related that the funeral took place two days after his death.

'It was attended by his two sergeants, NCOs & 21 of his comrades. A cross marks the spot. Everything that we could do was done for him; he was esteemed by us all'.

Capt H Collinson, his chaplain, in sending condolences, stated that *'He was killed bravely doing his duty'*.

The massed battle traffic of an advance by British troops near Cambrai, where Lance Corporal Arthur Odell was fighting shortly before his death.

Just off the road between Cambrai and Peronne lies the village of Fins. Lance Corporal Arthur Odell, G/15640, 13th Battalion Royal Sussex Regiment was buried at the nearby Fins New British Cemetery, Sorel-Le-Grand Somme, France (Ref IV.C.10). His name is also on the memorial at All Saints Church Hertford to the dead of the 1st Hertfordshire Regiment. The local newspaper reported:

'He was one of the nine Pirton boys in the first contingent of Herts Regiment to go to France in August 1914. There are few left now; three we believe.'

A monument inscription in St. Mary's churchyard in the village reads: *'Our dear boys Pte Frederick Odell, died of wounds 23 April 1919 aged 19, also Lce/Cpl Arthur Odell, killed in action in France 26 February 1918 aged 21'.*

Mary and John's oldest son, James, served on a Royal Navy destroyer – and survived - whilst at the time of Arthur's death, their youngest son Fred, then 19, had just joined the Royal Fusiliers. He was to die of terrible war wounds fourteen months later.

Soldier 20: Died Sunday 24th March 1918

LANCE SERGEANT CHARLES WILSHERE
ONE OF THE OLDEST PIRTON SOLDIERS KILLED

Whilst many of the men on our memorial were little more than lads, the battlefields of North-West Europe had no regard for age. Charles Wilshere was forty when he was killed somewhere on the bloody fields of northern France.

Gathering together the story of Charles Wilshere, even a fragmented one, was more difficult than with many of the Pirton victims. Firstly, there is confusion over the surname, variously spelt Wilshere, Wilsher, Wilshire and Willshere. *(The spelling on the Village War Memorial is used in this article).* Secondly, whilst many of his family remained in Pirton, Charles moved away from the village and seems to have lost his main ties with Pirton. In the final years of Victoria's reign, the expansion of building and other industries prompted Charles, like so many young men, to move to London. Employment in Pirton was meagre, for even the opportunity to be a poorly paid agricultural worker was declining, as machinery replaced men.

Whilst long distance travel was limited, there was always local movement between Pirton and surrounding villages. On 7th December 1873, James Wilshere, born in Lilley, married Sarah Larman, born and bred in Pirton. In 1871 Sarah, aged 19, had been a strawplaiter living with her brother in law, Joseph Chamberlain and his wife Mary, in Wet Lane. When married, Sarah and James settled in Pirton and over the next sixteen years they had six children – Martha (born in 1875), Charles (1878), Frederick (1882), Robert (1885), Arthur (1887) and Bertram (Bertie) (1890).

It is the progress of their second child, Charles, we now follow. Another poor village family, they moved around the village to wherever accommodation could be found; often dependent upon the farmer with whom James could find any work. Over the next few years they lived variously 'near the pond', 'downtown' and 'Wet Lane'.

The opening of the school in 1877 was one of the biggest events in the history of Pirton. Clearing the rough ground, brick walls slowly rising and then the roof and windows being put in place had generated huge interest among the villagers. Some knew that the school would change the life of the young children and future generations in a major way. Charles started at the school when he was three, the school only in its fourth year. His siblings followed him and over the next few years Wilsher(e)s appears frequently on the school roll.

By the time Charles left the school, the family was living in Wet Lane, (now West Lane) - probably one of the five cottages opposite the Holwell end of Royal Oak Lane, which were later burnt down.

In the late 1890's there had became quite an 'ex-Pirton stronghold' in north London. The attraction was generated by employment as 'gangers' on the railway, based in Finsbury Park. The line from Hitchin was direct and an increasing number of Pirton men worked and stayed in north London from Monday to Saturday lunchtime, returning to the village for the rest of the weekend. So strong was the Finsbury Park contingent, that Revd. Langmore wrote that he hoped copies of the Pirton parish magazine would go to *'our colony in Finsbury Park'*.

On leaving Pirton, Charles joined this Finsbury Park 'colony'. However, in 1894 Clara, an aunt to Charles, who had been living with the extended family running the 'Shoulder of Mutton' pub in Hambridge Way, moved with her husband Thomas to London. By 1901 they were living at 169 Cornelia Street in the Lower Holloway region of Islington and Charles, now 23 and a

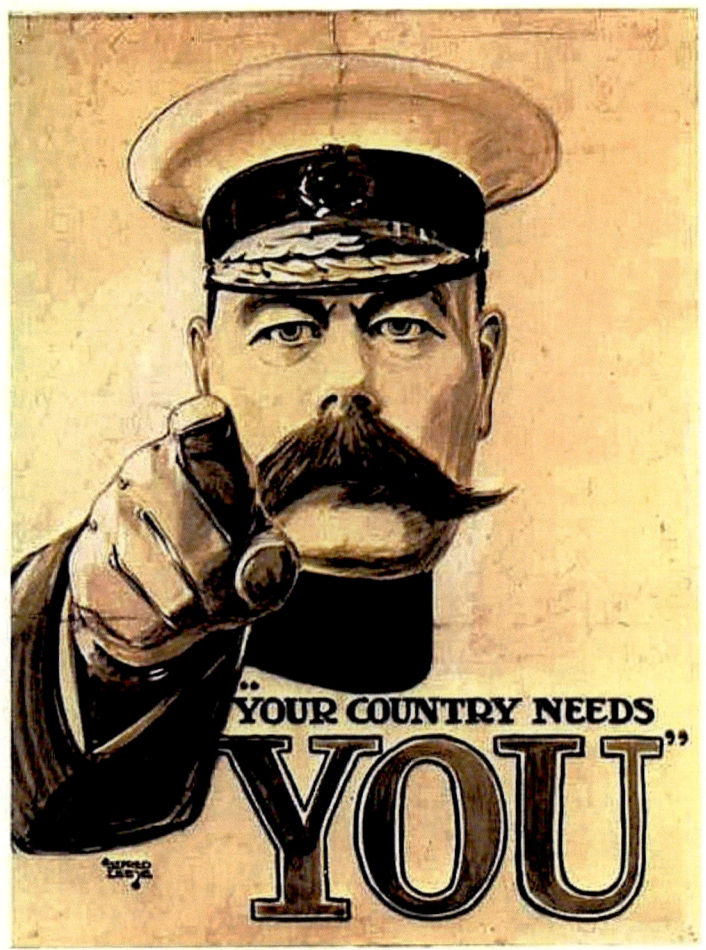

The poster portraying Secretary of State for War, Lord Kitchener, had a huge impact in its appeal to the nation's men to fight.

'general labourer', was boarding with them. So, too, was Frederick Goldsmith formerly from Little Green, in Pirton. This had become another small London colony of Pirton villagers.

Charles' life over the next decade remains unknown, but he seems to have continued living and working in North London. During this first decade of the new century the clouds of an oncoming war slowly gathered. By 1915, posters informing every passer-by that 'Your Country Needs You' were abundant. On 18th May of that year, the 21st Battalion Middlesex regiment was formed by the Mayor in the Borough of Islington. This may well have been when Charles joined up; he certainly enlisted in Holloway with service number G/15042.

Sadly, many service records of these war years were destroyed by bombing in the Second World War, thus details of numerous men have been lost forever. By 1915, Charles was 37 and he was soon promoted to Corporal. Also fighting for their King and Country were Charles' younger brothers, Frederick, Arthur and Bertie.

In the spring of 1917, Charles was on hospital leave recovering from an injury that had taken place on Easter Monday. On 14th April, five days later, the bullet was removed at the First Australian General Hospital. He wrote,

'We were advancing when the Germans let the machine guns go and I got a bullet. It went in at the top of the buttock and stopped just above the back of the knee. Much better now. Nothing to worry about'.

Two of his brothers were back in England with war injuries. Frederick was awaiting discharge after a leg was amputated, Arthur less seriously injured; only Bert remained at the Front.

Charles recovered, at least physically, and returned to this *'war to end all wars'*. He was now Lance Sergeant Charles Wilshere G/15042. By March 1918 the Western Front ran from Ypres southwards to Saint-Quentin and beyond. Whilst details of individuals' whereabouts in this long line are unknown, it is well recorded that on 21st March, exceptionally heavy German shellfire hit many areas of the British front with the main weight of attack between Arras and a few miles south of Saint-Quentin. British losses were particularly heavy during the next few days.

Charles was killed on 24th March 1918. The circumstances of his death are not known, his body never identified. In a local newspaper report of 4th May (five weeks after his death) Lance Sergeant Charles Wilshere and two other Pirton men, Charles Titmuss and Bert Wilson, were reported as missing. A further four months on, it was stated that '*news was anxiously awaited*'.

This protracted anxiety, culminating in grief, touched the hearts of many in those Pirton enclaves in North London and in the village itself. This was the period of the war when almost every home in Pirton seemed affected by telegrams carrying news of a death, or letters bearing love to wife, sweetheart or friend. The village's suffering seemed to be never-ending, for yet more were to die in the remaining months of the war.

Charles is commemorated on the Arras Memorial at Pas de Calais in France (Bay 7) as Charles Wilsher.

Although there is no evidence that he married, there are still family connections with him in Pirton. The variation of surname is well revealed:

> Maureen Worsley who lives in Davis Crescent Pirton is the granddaughter of Bertram Wilsher, brother of Charles.

> Pat Pickering, who lives in Holwell Road Pirton, is the daughter of Bertram Wilsher.

> Pete Wilshere of Shillington Road Pirton is the grandson of another brother.

Some family connections are complicated, not least because first cousins sometimes married, both descending from the same family, but with differently spelt family names.

Charles' sister Martha married her first cousin, Abraham John Willsher, also from Pirton, when he returned from the Boer War. Two of their grandchildren, Pat Trafford and Colin Willsher, have helped verify much of the family detail.

Lance Sergeant Charles Wilshere is commemorated at the Arras Memorial where almost 35,000 servicemen from the United Kingdom, South Africa and New Zealand who have no known grave, are remembered. Three other Pirton men are also commemorated there.

Soldier 21: Died Wednesday 27th March 1918

PRIVATE BERT WILSON

SON OF MARTHA, THE 'VILLAGE MEDICINE LADY'

Like so many victims of the Great War, little is known about Bert Wilson. He was one of the millions from the under-privileged; working classes plunged into a war of mud, blood and death. But it was not only those killed whose lives were savaged by the war. Martha Wilson, Bert's mother, struggled to keep her family going, saw him torn away from her in a conflict of which she had no part and then tried to piece her life back together.

Much is heard in present-day society of single parents; this was not uncommon in Pirton a century and more ago. Whether or not Bert Wilson knew the identity of his father is unknown, certainly it is not shown on his birth or baptismal record.

Martha Matilda Wilson was among the poorest, first earning a pittance as a straw plaiter and washerwoman, later as 'the medicine lady of Pirton'. Yet her ability to survive showed immense enterprise as she turned her hand to various jobs. For Bert Wilson, his life of twenty-four years passed unrecorded and largely unrecognised; it is only with his death that history makes significant mention of him.

Martha, born in the first part of 1872**, was the second daughter of James and Hannah Wilson (nee Titmuss), whose families had been in Pirton for generations. By the time Martha was eight, she had three young sisters – Sarah, Ellen and Emma. All were to take up one of the few jobs in the village, working from home as strawplaiters, supplying the Luton hat-making industry. Martha's only brother Charles, struggled unsuccessfully with the demands of education; on the 1901 census he is recorded as *'an imbecile'*, later earning a crust as a *'jobbing labourer'*.

Martha, when twenty-two, gave birth to her only child, baptized at St. Mary's on the 13th May 1894 as Bertram William Newbery Wilson. There is no named father, although one wonders if his third name, Newbery, a not uncommon name in the village, gives a clue to his parentage.

While still a youngster, Bert, his mother, two aunts (Ellen and Emma) and his Uncle Charlie moved to what is now number 79 High Street. Life was exceedingly hard in a time when there were no state benefits. Martha earned what she could as a washerwoman, but was always on the look-out for other jobs in the village. Uncle Charlie was only able to do the most simple jobs and Ellen and Emma took any unskilled work that was going. After leaving school around 1907, Bert worked on the land and did some odd-

Photographed a century year on, Martha Wilson's home in High Street is now much changed and more attractive.

jobbing. The future was rather bleak and so it was probably with a sense of relief, as well as some excitement, when, just 21, he enlisted on 2nd March 1915. He had a real identity, Wilson, Bertram W N Private 23187, 4th Battalion, Bedfordshire Regiment. He first served at the 4th Bedfordshire's Training Deport before being transferred to the 8th Battalion.

Of his war experiences little is known. Letters, if there were any between the family members, have not survived. Bert was typical of the many young men thrown into a European-wide conflict when mere survival at home would have been a challenge. He had exchanged a life of drudgery for a harrowing and fearful experience in France and Flanders. No doubt his mother, Martha, amidst all her work in keeping the family home going, feared for her only child.

In March 1918 the Germans with over three million men, mounted a huge assault on British lines around Arras. Over 80,000 British became prisoners of war. Chaos and confusion reigned throughout the British lines and reports of gains or losses, never mind individual casualties, were often inaccurate.

It is recorded that Private Wilson was *'killed in action on Wednesday 27th March 1918'*. It is unknown when Martha received the grim news that her only son was dead. In a local newspaper report of 2nd May (five weeks after his death) three Pirton men were reported as missing: Charles Titmuss, Bertram Wilson and Charles Wilshere. Later, in August 1918, that Bert was a prisoner of war and still later that *'news is anxiously awaited'*. In fact, of the missing three only Charles Titmuss was a prisoner; Bert, along with Charles Wilshere was dead. The anonymity of Bert in life seemed equalled by that in death, for in the August 1918 parish magazine's list of men whose names were to go on *'Our War Shrine'*, his was not included (five months after his death).

Thus his mother, his aunts, Uncle Charlie and friends were for several months bewildered by confusing news. The sheer volume of deaths prevented even human grief running a natural course.

Private Bertram Wilson is commemorated on the Arras Memorial, Pas de Calais, France (Bay 5) along with 35,000 other men who died in the Arras sector. One of these men was older fellow villager, Charles Wilshere who had died just three days earlier. Indeed, two other Pirton men who had died in fighting near Arras eleven months earlier, Privates George Trussell and Joseph Handscombe are also commemorated on the Arras Memorial.

One of the many areas where thousands of shells churned up the fields into an unbelievable sea of mud. The only way that the men might possibly move about was along the duckboards that are seen stretching into the distance. Men and horses often drowned without trace in such places.

Having passed through life without great note, in death Private Bert Wilson was to be commemorated four times in Pirton; on the Village War Memorial, in St. Mary's, the Methodist Chapel and at the village school.

Now we turn to the story of his mother, Martha, for she forms part of the village's history, almost folklore. Several years after her son's death, Martha found a partner, Abraham Weeden a ploughman of Pirton birth. At the insistence of the Rev. Thomas Winkworth, Martha and Abraham were married. Remarkably, Grace Maidment now living in Shillington Road, but then a few doors from the Martha and Abraham's house, recalls the wedding. She can remember that during the celebrations, Abraham sang as a solo *'Martha Matilda, the watercress girl.'*

Martha took on a new role in the 1920s and into the 30s. Most villagers were registered with Dr William Grellett, a Hitchin doctor, and many subscribed to a regular 'Doctors' Club' which paid for prescriptions and treatment. Villagers brought their repeat prescription bottles to Martha's home and every Tuesday and Saturday she pushed a pram with all the empty bottles to the Hitchin surgery. With bottles refilled, Martha dressed in her long black skirt, straw bonnet and tiny buttoned boots, would push the pram back on the three mile journey to the village. She would be seen on the track from Hitchin, followed by her brother Charlie and husband Abby. It was often Charlie who would take the medicine to villagers' homes, collecting twopence for delivering the medicines and threepence for the 'Doctors' Club' papers. Every Christmas, Dr Grellet came to the village and gave Martha a pair of new boots.

There is no monumental inscription in St, Mary's churchyard for Martha, although it would seem that she, Abraham and Charlie are buried there. To the humble Bert, his name is inscribed on the Village War Memorial; just one of millions who died in *'the war to end all wars'*. Memorials seem to have been the only record of his life. Maybe Bertolt Brecht's words from *'A Mother to her Soldier Son'* could be ascribed to Bert:

> *'Now as you go forth to do your master's bloody business, in front of you the enemy guns, at your back the officer's pistol, remember, their defeat is not yours, and neither is their victory.'*

From the time of Private Bert Wilson's death, the frequency of Pirton casualties was to gain an awful momentum.

A weathered panel on the Village War Memorial records the name of a seemingly anonymous man, until he gave his life in the war.

** *Martha's birth year appears on the parish records as 1872, but on a census as 1874. The former has been assumed as the most likely.*

Soldier 22: Died Saturday 20th April 1918

PRIVATE HENRY CHAMBERLAIN

PIRTON'S TOUGH GUY - WINNER OF A MAJOR BRAVERY AWARD

> ### NEWS STORY
>
> *'Exciting night scenes at Pirton', read the Hitchin newspaper headline in October, 1914. Appearing at the Hitchin sessions, a Pirton man was found guilty of hitting two Pirton special constables outside the White Horse (now the Motte & Bailey) and later that night of assaulting Ellen Hubbard, after she sprang to the defence of her husband. 'A most serious charge' said the chairman of the court. Total fines of £3.7s.6d were imposed or six weeks in prison on failure to pay.*
>
> *The assailant was Henry George Chamberlain; George Charlick (senior) was one of the special constables assaulted.*
>
> *Four years later, the assailant Henry Chamberlain and George Charlick, son of the constable who made the arrest, were both killed in France.*

Young Henry Chamberlain

There doesn't seem much doubt that Henry George Chamberlain was one of the village's 'tough guys'. He was born in the autumn of 1878, son of twenty-two year old Rose, one of the three known children of Thomas and Dinah Chamberlain. Rose had a younger sister, Elizabeth, who was to play a major role in Henry's life.

Henry was baptized at St. Mary's on Christmas Day 1878; his mother having been baptised on Christmas Day, twenty two years previously. Rose was another single parent and in times when many children had to take on adult roles, much of the responsibility for Henry's upbringing fell on her sister Elizabeth, who was only twelve when Henry was born.

Life was hard; money was short and young Elizabeth, growing up before the days of any compulsory education, earned the little she could delivering a few newspapers in the village. For this, she had to walk the two miles to Shillington to collect the papers and then, pushing Henry in the pram, would take the newspapers around the village. Sometimes she had to speak firmly to young Henry who seemed to delight in ripping up the papers!

Aged only 38, Rose died in 1895, and sixteen year old Henry lived in his Aunt Elizabeth's house, in what was known as Andrews Row or Pudding Bag Lane, now part of West Lane. Henry probably saw Elizabeth as his mother figure for most of his early life, even before his mother died.

He attended Pirton School and then, following most of his school friends, became an agricultural worker, relying on seasonal money. His aunt continued with the newspaper round, earning some extra shillings as a straw plaiter. In 1896, Elizabeth married Frederick Gazeley; they had two children, (Mary) Rose and Frederick Thomas, who shared the small cottage with twenty-two year old Henry. Sadly, Elizabeth's husband died in 1904.

Henry's life continued with hard, poorly paid work; the only excitement likely to be in nearby Hitchin or a night out with the boys in one of the local pubs. As the war years loomed, Henry was working for James Walker at Little Green Farm near the village pond. It was in the early months of the war, before Henry joined the army, that he had the fracas with the two special constables, Messers Bertram Walker and George Charlick, outside the White Horse. Henry's punishment, meted out by the chairman of the bench, F.A. Delme-Radcliffe, was substantial. His fine was a heavy one for a poorly paid farm worker; whether or not he paid it or went to prison by default is not known.

In June 1915, Henry volunteered and joined the Suffolk Bantam Brigade, a brigade raised at Bury St. Edmunds. So many British soldiers were required in the first full year of the war that the Government lowered its height specifications for soldiers and established 'Bantam' battalions for men under 5 feet 3 inches tall. These 'Bantam' soldiers sometimes encountered difficulties (i.e. with the weight of weapons and depth of trenches). However, though Henry was short of stature and slightly built, his aggressive spirit made up for his lack of inches. He became Henry George Chamberlain, Private 20655, 2nd Battalion, Suffolk Regiment.

He had soon left the peace and quiet of Pirton, probably fulfilling his innermost wishes, and was in France from May 1916. His village toughness changed to battle-front bravado and in 1917 he was to become Pirton's most highly decorated soldier – the Distinguished Conduct Medal, for *'Acts of extraordinary bravery'*. This was a medal for sergeants and other ranks, but it was unusual for it to be gained by a private.

His toughness from village fights was used to advantage in war and he always seemed to be in the thick of battle. During one action he was badly injured and rendered unconscious, returning to England early in 1917. But in July of the same year, he returned to the Front and on 23rd October, the London Gazette reported his extraordinary deeds that gained him the coveted Distinguished Conduct Medal, a gallantry award second only to the Victoria Cross.

'Entirely on his own initiative he went in search of a German sniper and found three in a shell-hole. He killed them and returned with Very lights and a trench lamp. He afterwards accounted for three more snipers. He was further instrumental in the capture of a pill-box containing twelve Huns who had been overlooked by the front line troops. He also bayoneted several Germans who feigned death.'

Distinguished Conduct Medal

This was the stuff of war and the local press acclaimed his feats with great nationalistic passion. *'This brave lad's achievement is the pride of Pirton's war traditions, being the highest honour accorded a village resident.'* There was further heroic writing in the local paper of 2nd May, *'The gallant boys of Pirton are surely adding to the military glory of the village'*. His activity in a tract of no-man's land at Zonnebeke near Ypres, where he stalked Germans with a singular intent to kill, must have spread round his home village as it had in the trenches.

The Parish Magazine was more modest, but understandably proud of this Pirton man's honour: *'We congratulate Private Henry Chamberlain on having won the DCM in Flanders. The G.O.C. praised him for his gallant conduct and splendid pluck.'*

RM Stevenson, Staff Captain, wrote: *'The General Officer commanding the Brigade sends you hearty congratulations on winning the DCM for your very gallant conduct at Zonnebeke. You earned it well by your pluck'.*

Sadly, tough and brave though this 39 year old Pirton man was, his luck ran out. Whilst the circumstances are unknown, on Saturday 20th April 1918, Henry died of wounds received in battle in the area of Pernes-en-Artois, a small town on the main road from Lillers to St Pol in France. With a severe wound in the head and fractured skull, Henry was admitted into a Canadian Casualty Clearing Station. He was partly conscious, but died shortly after being brought in. The Chaplain writing on 23rd April; said *'We buried him in the cemetery near by with a number of other brave comrades'*. He concludes, *'We have been having a dreadful time'*.

He was buried at Pernes British Cemetery, France. (Ref. I..C. 2). This was not started until April 1918, when the 1st and 4th Canadian Casualty Clearing Stations came to Pernes. His grave bears the words: *"God is love in paradise"*.

To his Aunt Elizabeth, who had acted as a parent to Henry, his cousins Rose and Fred Gazeley, and to all his village mates it was a time for sadness. To the whole village the burden of sorrow grew at an even greater pace and intensity.

So Private Henry George Chamberlain became another name for the Village War Memorial, the only one bearing the DCM. What became of the medal itself? It may have been presented to his Aunt Elizabeth, and around 1925 one of her children, Rose Gazeley emigrated to Australia. However, her Australian descendents have never seen the medal and Fred Gazeley (junior), living on Great Green, never remembers his father speaking of the medal and he, too, wonders where it is now.

Pernes British Cemetery, the final resting place for Private Henry Chamberlain, DCM.

Soldier 23 : Died Monday 17th June 1918

PRIVATE GEORGE CHARLICK

LONDON BORN, SON OF PIRTON SPECIAL CONSTABLE

George Charlick was a Middlesex man; it was through his parents' move to their adopted village of Pirton, that his name is on the Village War Memorial. His own links with the village remain uncertain but were, perhaps, no more than visits to his family. Relatively little is known of the man himself.

By the 1880s, the population of London was rapidly extending into the countryside, and Enfield was one of the many expanding communities in Middlesex. It was there, at 3 Cleveland Terrace (off Totteridge Road), that George Thomas** Charlick was born in the summer of 1887; a time of national excitement as the Queen had just celebrated her Golden Jubilee.

His father, after whom he carried the same first Christian name, was 26 when young George was born. His mother, Elizabeth, had been born in Bedford of Irish lineage. George Junior was the eldest of three children. Alfred, an uncle to young George was also living with the family. Both father and uncle worked at the local Royal Small Arms Company at Enfield Lock. This was the company that produced the Lee-Enfield rifle in 1907 which became the British Army's main infantry weapon.

Some time in the next ten years, the family moved to Essex, close to the boundary with Kent. By 1901, George Charlick Snr. had changed his work and part-owned a public house, probably the Hare and Groom in Warley Road close to Brentwood, where the family lived. By this time, when George was thirteen, he had a brother Ernest and a sister, Lily May (always known as May).

George Charlick Snr. continued his role as a publican, first back in Enfield and then moving to Cambridgeshire, taking over the Hare and Hounds public house in Eynesbury near St. Neots. The next move for George Snr. and his wife Elizabeth was to Pirton living at 'Syringa', one of the several old cottages in Royal Oak Lane (now number 14). This was sometime before 1914 and was to be their home for the rest of their lives. Having finished with his public house days, George now took on the role of special constable and he was one of two constables assaulted by later war-hero Henry Chamberlain. Four years on, the assailant, Henry Chamberlain, and George Charlick, son of the constable

The Charlick family lived only a short distance from the Small Arms Factory at Enfield Lock. George Snr worked there. The factory's production was to have a significant role in the ensuing war.

George continued living in London when his parents moved to Pirton. It was outside the White Horse that Henry Chamberlain had a fracas with George Snr, special constable.

making the arrest, were both dead; their names later to be inscribed next to each other on the Village War Memorial.

Late in 1915, in addition to his duties as a special constable, George Snr. was one of the canvassing officers who contacted some eighty non-serving men in Pirton as a way of increasing the number of men joining up. Set up by Lord Derby, the new Director-General of Recruitment, the 'Derby Scheme' enabled men aged 18 to 40 to continue to enlist voluntarily, or attest with an obligation to do so if called upon, with the promise that married men would be called last. At the same time, a war pension was introduced to help entice men concerned about supporting their dependants. The villagers who attested were sent back to their homes and jobs until they were called up, wearing a grey armband with a red crown as a sign that they had volunteered.

Of George's childhood little is known. Three years before the outbreak of the war, George seems to have been working in a Westminster pub, appropriately called 'The Speaker'. The fact that George Jnr. joined the London Regiment, probably living in Rosebery Avenue Tottenham at the time, suggests he was just a visitor to Pirton. He does not appear to have married.

He enlisted in Holborn as Private George Charlick, 2/11th London Regiment. This 2nd/11th (County of London) Battalion, known as the Finsbury Rifles had been formed in London in September 1914. However, the London regiment was a loose collection of territorial battalions, rather than a standard infantry regiment and changes between battalions were common; later the battalion joined the 175th Brigade, 58th Division. Private George Charlick got caught up in the many changes of personnel as more men were killed and needed replacing. At some stage of the war, he became Private George Charlick, service no. 698133 of the $1^{st}/22^{nd}$ Battalion, London Regiment.

On one of his home leaves to his parents' home in Pirton, George was persuaded by his younger brother, Ernest, to give a first hand demonstration of his military prowess. Ernest, his brother, shouted *'Attention'*! George held his rifle up as to attention, but his rifle went off sending a bullet into the ceiling, much to the consternation of all present. Perhaps, there is still a bullet buried in the ceiling of number 14!

Of his war-time activity, one can only relate the engagements of his regiment, with whom Private George Charlick served. In 1917, he was likely to have been at Ypres, in June the Messines Ridge and five months later in the fighting at Bourlon Wood. As the war moved deeper into 1918, mistakes and oversights in the Allies' commands enabled the Germans to make advances unlike any since the first autumn of the war. In the area around Metz-en-Couture, battles were again fought over already shell-torn land. In Aveluy Wood, where Private Charlick probably fought, the wood is still scarred by the British trenches.

Whatever the detail of George's battles, he was killed in action near the Somme on 17th June 1918. In the cottages in Royal Oak Lane, war deaths were no stranger. Next door to Elizabeth and George Charlick, the Odells had already lost one son; another to die a few months later.

Private George Charlick is commemorated on the Pozieres Memorial, Somme, France (panel 89). This impressive memorial commemorates over 14,000 casualties of the United Kingdom and 300 of the South African Forces who have no known grave and who died on the Somme between 21st March and 7th August 1918. He was one of the thousands of war-worn men driven back by overwhelming numbers of the German army across the former Somme battlefields. Tragically, he was dead by the time of the *'Advance to Victory'* which commenced on 8th August. Pozieres, from which a long, straight road leads to his memorial, is a village some six kilometres north-east of Albert.

If the time between an unidentified death and the news reaching those back in England followed its normal course, it is likely that Private George Charlick's parents may have been ignorant of their son's tragic death until the war was over.

However, the pain of so many deaths of Pirton men, and the numbing effect upon their families, had already touched Mr and Mrs Charlick. In the month before their son was killed, they had made a donation to the memorial to be erected in the village.

Elizabeth and George stayed in Pirton for the rest of their lives. Their remaining son, Ernest Nugent Charlick, became a policeman and years later in preparation for his retirement, built a house on the edge of the village, Northmead in Holwell Road. Ernest and his wife Minnie had a daughter called Una. After Minnie died, Ernest sold the house, in July 1946, to Margot and Michael Anderson. Ernest then lodged at 16 Royal Oak Lane with Dora Walker, whom he later married. This was next door to his childhood home. Ernest died in 1967, the last known member of the Charlick family living in the village.

George senior (died 1929), his wife Elizabeth (died 1945) and Ernest Nugent and his first wife (died 1943) are all buried in St. Mary's churchyard.

In the transcription of the 1911 census, he is referred to as Harry George Charlick. This is the only known reference to this first Christian name.

George Charlick is commemorated on the Pozieres Memorial. It commemorates over 14,000 casualties of the United Kingdom and 300 South African Forces who have no known grave and who died on the Somme from the 21st March to the 7th August 1918.

Soldier 24: Died Monday 8th July 1918

PRIVATE FREDERICK ANDERSON

DECLARED UNFIT, HE LABOURS ON AND DIES OF PNEUMONIA

The men usually died with gun in hand, but for Private Fred Anderson it was different. Fighting from 1915, but then declared unfit for the Front Line, he was transferred to the Labour Corps. Armed with a shovel, not a gun, he laboured on until he became so sick that hospitalisation was essential; some while later he died of pneumonia. His time with the Labour Corps reveals something of the relatively unknown story of that branch of the army; 9,000 men in the Labour Corps were to die supporting the fighting soldiers.

Private Frederick Anderson is one of the four names on the Village War Memorial of men not born in the village. He was from a family who had for years lived and worked around the hamlet of Norton, later to become part of Letchworth Garden City. Fred's grandfather and John, his father, were agricultural workers on Wilbury Farm, between Norton and Ickleford. Fred, born in 1883, was the second child of John and Elizabeth Anderson, with an older sister Margaret and Minnie, who was five years his junior. Fred's mother seems to have died in childbirth when Minnie was born.

Life was hard for John, bringing up the family on his own. On leaving school, Fred followed the same route as most young men in North Hertfordshire villages, working on the land. He moved from the family home to a farm at Willian, on the other side of the newly emerging Letchworth Garden City, lodging in one of the Lordship Farm cottages with John and Elizabeth Harper and their son Charles.

Living next door was the Worbey family and, towards the end of 1905 Fred, then 22, married Lillian Lizzie Worbey. A few years before her marriage, she and her older brother John had tried their luck, moving to Tunstall in Staffordshire.

Fred Anderson was born on a farm and, like many lads leaving school in North Hertfordshire, stayed in farming until he joined up.

There they worked in the potteries, possibly with the famous Wedgwood Company, but she had later returned to Willian.

Lillian and Fred were married and were soon living at one of the High Down cottages on the edge of Pirton. In the late summer of 1909, they were thrilled by the arrival of a daughter, Winifred.

A year later, Fred was working for Thomas Franklin of Walnut Tree Farm. The Franklins were a good family to work for, as shown in October 1911 when Thomas Franklin organised a harvest supper for his employees with the food provided by Mr Cooper of the Angel Vaults in Hitchin. Following the meal (and plenty of drink one may assume) and after the usual loyal toasts came the singing of some old-fashioned English songs, sung with great gusto. Five of the farm workers joined forces in the singing, including Fred Anderson along with David Titmuss, Ernest and George Males and Harry Crawley; the latter also to die in the fast-approaching war.

Fred's work with Thomas Franklin was such that he was promoted to farm bailiff at the High Down farm.

However, these days of peace and tilling the soil, albeit also of hard work and poor pay, soon gave way to the clamour for war. Fred was over thirty when, sometime before September 1915, he joined the 8th Battalion of the Bedfordshire Regiment as Private Frederick Anderson, 18618. The 8th saw much action, serving in both France and Flanders. In early 1917, Fred was attached to a tunnelling company in the Royal Engineers. This work was extremely hazardous, the men often tunnelling at great depth under the enemy and planting explosives. Fred was injured and invalided home. When partially recovered and deemed no longer fit for the Front, he found himself a member of the Labour Corps.

At the start of the war, tasks such as moving stores, repairing roads and building defences were carried out by soldiers when they were rested from the Front. As the war progressed, far more men were needed in the trenches, and periods of rest became ever shorter as the war-weary men were hurried back to the Front.

This meant that the Army was short of a labour force, but a 'solution' was soon found by the army commanders. In 1917, the British Army's Labour Corps was formed. This Corps was manned by men who were either ex-front line soldiers who had been wounded, or taken ill, or men who on enlistment were found to be unfit for front line service. In the crisis on the Western Front, during March and April 1918, they were even used as emergency infantry, suffering from lack of transport, inexperienced officers and colleagues of a pitiful physical grade. By the end of the war the Labour Corps numbered nearly 390,000 men (more than 10% of the total size of the Army).

Early in 1918, he was transferred to the 141st Company, Labour Corps. This company had been formed mainly from the 3rd Infantry Labour Company, Northamptonshire Regiment, but Private Fred Anderson and many others were added.

He would have been given any labouring task required; building and repairing roads and railways, building defences, laying electricity and telephones cables, moving ammunition and stores and burying the dead. Some companies worked unarmed within the range of German guns; often for weeks or even months at a time with only one day's rest a week.

It is likely that in the first two months of 1918, Fred was part of the 141st Company at the Westhoek Light Railway in Picardy and, with the 145CLC (Chinese Labour Corps Company), at Flavy Le Martel. The Chinese Labour Corps has been virtually hidden from war records, but it was a significant part of the labouring force. From March 1917, Chinese men were employed in digging trenches, building other defences and transporting projects. However, the political masters in London did not want a re-emergence of the 'Chinese Slavery' scandal of the Boer War. Many were from London and Liverpool and other parts of the Empire. Lloyd George had a plan for moving thousands from Hong Kong, but that never came to fruition. Noyelles-sur-Mer, at the Somme estuary, was the base depot of the Chinese Labour Corps in France. By 1918,

The needs of the war caused many nationalities to be involved. Private Fred Anderson almost certainly worked with many of the Chinese in the Labour Corps.

100,000 men were involved; nearly 2000 died.

Thus, with the grouping of the 141st Company and the 145th Chinese Labour Corps, Fred Anderson almost certainly worked alongside many Chinese men.

In May 1918, the 141st were involved in working on GHQ defences at Camblain and, as that is in the region of Pas de Calais (where he was later to be buried), it is likely that it was there, that he was taken ill. He was probably hospitalised at no. 42 or no. 57 Casualty Clearing Station which were based near Aubigny.

Private Frederick Anderson's wife, Lillian, received a telegram at her Hitchin home informing her that her husband was dangerously ill. Over many months he had suffered several injuries and illness and on Monday 8th July 1918 he succumbed to pneumonia. He is buried in the Aubigny Communal cemetery extension at Pas de Calais (IV J 41), fifteen kilometres north of Arras. The extension cemetery contains 2,771 burials of Commonwealth men from the First World War.

It is not known what happened to Lillian his wife or Winifred their daughter who, at the time of Private Fred Anderson's death, were living at 5 Periwinkle Lane in Hitchin.

Looking at the War Memorial by St. Mary's Church in the market town of Hitchin, only four miles from Pirton, one can read his name. Living in Hitchin and working in Pirton rightly justifies Private Frederick Anderson to be remembered in both places.

Gunner Fred Anderson's name is also on the War Memorial set in front of the beautiful Hitchin church of St. Mary's The inset shows his name on the first of 11 panels, totalling 356 names in all.

Soldier 25: Died Friday 9th August 1918

GUNNER ALBERT REYNOLDS

A NATURE LOVER – EVEN IN TIME OF WAR

Mary and Lewis Reynolds had long feared for their sons; six of them were at war and news was patchy, sometimes absent altogether. The growing number of casualties from Pirton, with the accompanying clouds of despair descending on this poor but tight-knit community, had reached a low for Mary and Lewis, when their youngest son Walter was killed in December 1917. The local newspaper might sing the praises of the Reynolds boys, *'Few families can show a better record of war service'* – but they were their children. Only eight months after the death of Walter, came the hammer-blow with the death of another of their sons – Gunner Albert Reynolds.

Albert, born in November 1884, was the seventh of the thirteen surviving children of Lewis Reynolds, the Pirton chimney sweep and his wife Mary, who turned her hand to straw plaiting in between bearing children. Young Albert spent hours playing and working in the fields and woods surrounding the village and developed an abiding interest in nature, turning this knowledge to good effect when he left school. Years later he kept a diary and, amid the awfulness of the battlefields, noted *'the heavy dew... the rooks building their nests... the bumble bees whirling past...the nightingale'*.

Soon after leaving school in 1897, Albert went to Kings Walden, living with his eldest brother, Jacob and wife, Martha. They had a young daughter, Alice. He worked as a domestic groom in that village, but in time he left his brother's home and worked as gamekeeper for Alfred Payne, foreman at Shillington Manor. Often he walked the three miles to the Pirton family home at no. 3 Wesley Cottages (now behind the Village Stores), but for much of that time, he lived in the servants' quarters at 'The Manor'.

It was there that the eye of this handsome, rugged man fell on Caroline Bashford, a young cook

from a Lancashire family. Albert then took on a job in the Croydon area. It was there that they married in the early summer of 1907 and the following year, Caroline gave birth to a son, Alfred John Louis. By 1911 they were living in Chertsey in a lodge off Hills Road. There was to be one more move for the family, some seven miles to Windlesham in Surrey. Their home at Laurel Cottage, one of a number of terraced cottages, (now 2 Kennel Lane) probably belonged to a nearby estate where Albert worked as a game-keeper and stock-keeper.

Much of this part of Surrey with its rolling heathland had become a major area for establishing army camps in the nineteenth century, with the Royal Military Academy at nearby Camberley. It was there that Albert joined up on 1st June 1916, becoming Gunner/Driver 90497 of the 139th Heavy Battery, Royal Garrison Artillery. The RGA was responsible for the heavy, large calibre guns and howitzers that were positioned some way behind the front line.

During the rest of 1916, Albert was training at

From a young age, Albert Reynolds will have explored around the village and Millway (later Hambridge Way) was a popular walk. The 'Shoulder of Mutton', later burnt down, a favourite stopping place.

Dover, but on 18th January 1917 he left Aldershot for France, landing at Le Havre on 19th January and reaching the French town of Albert, two days later.

He kept a diary, which was later returned to his wife. The diary was used by Rev. Alfred Hutton, then Rector of St John the Baptist Church Windlesham. When the town's War Memorial was being erected in the early 1920s, he wrote about the WW1 victims. Thus, Albert Reynolds name is inscribed there, as well as at Pirton.

The diary extracts tell only a little about Gunner Albert Reynolds's war campaign, more about his thinking during these terrible times. In the first part of 1917 he spent time in Dunkirk, St Omer and Rouen. Injuries from wartime accidents were commonplace, and on 19th July Albert suffered a fractured ankle, through a horse trampling on him, which necessitated going into hospital at St. Omer. After undergoing x-rays at Rouen, he went by the hospital ship St. George to Southampton and from there to the Killingbeck Hospital in Leeds. He was there until November when he went on home leave, reunited briefly with his wife Caroline and young son.

Whilst the war's focus was on Germany, there were troubles enough in Ireland. Albert was briefly transferred there, but not before he was able to take a short leave in Pirton. It was to be the last time he saw his parents who now had all of their sons in the army. In December 1917 his brother Walter was killed. One can only imagine Albert's distress at being unable to return to Pirton to console his parents.

Even under the shadow of war, his diary reflected Albert's love of nature. In England, waiting for the return to France he wrote:

'On 23rd March fine morning with heavy dew, the birds singing in the trees and the rooks building their nests. The sun was shining very hot towards the middle of the day; a butterfly was flying around and bumble bees were whirling past; thus ended a perfect day'.

On 13th April 1918 he left Winchester for France again and his diary extracts show he was in action on 25th April, when one of their company's guns was knocked out, and then for most of June and July. He must often have thought back to his peaceful youth around Pirton. In France, a diary entry on May 1st: *I heard the nightingale'*...

But these brief interludes into the magical way in which nature can be revealed, even among the torn shreds of shelled trees and crater-filled

Shells of the kind all too familiar to Gunner Albert Reynolds. Whilst these were under camouflage they were prone to both accident and enemy gunfire. Guns and shells simply got more destructive as the war went on.

fields, was soon to come to a tragic end. On 8th August he was probably with the British forces who attacked and, unusually, advanced six miles. Another soldier's diary reveals the horror of it all:

That night:

'It was utterly still. Vehicles made no sound on the marshy ground ... The silence played on our nerves a bit. As we got our guns into position you could hear drivers whispering to their horses and men muttering curses under their breath, and still the silence persisted, broken only by the whine of a stray rifle bullet or a long range shell passing high overhead ... we could feel that hundreds of groups of men were doing the same thing - preparing for the heaviest barrage ever launched.'

4.20 am the next day:

'All hell broke loose. The world was enveloped in sound and flame, and our ears just couldn't cope. The ground shook'.

After the initial advance, the resistance stiffened.

Somewhere in the fighting on that summer's day, in 1918, Albert Reynolds of sub-section E, Royal Garrison Artillery, was severely injured. *'Whilst lying in the makeshift hospital, he seemed to realize that his end was near'*, a colleague later wrote. Albert dictated a last letter to his wife Caroline. He died of his wounds the following day, Friday 9th August, and was buried in the Pernois British cemetery at Halloy-Les-Pernois, Somme (Ref. III. B. 14).

This seemingly gentle, country-loving man, devoted husband and father, was the twenty-fifth Pirton man to die in a war that seemed to go on for ever. It is well shown that he was considerate to all and made friends wherever he went.

The headstone in Pirton churchyard reads: *'Father & Mother & two sons sacrificed in the Great War'*. Of Albert's wife, Caroline and their son nothing is known. One wonders whether Gunner Albert Reynolds's diary was passed down by them, and is still to be discovered.

Soldier 26: Died Monday 9th September 1918

RIFLEMAN JACK PEARCE

PHYLLIS TELLS THE STORY OF HER TWO DEAD BROTHERS

To be sitting with a delightful 94-year old lady in her Pirton home hearing about her two brothers who were killed in the First World War, was an experience which will be long remembered. To realise that her life linked those war years with the present, brought an added poignancy to that tragic conflict. As the lives and deaths of the 30 Pirton men were researched, Phyllis Pearce had already talked about her brother Charlie Burton, who bore their mother's maiden name and was killed in December 1916. Now she recounted what she knew about another brother's death – Jack, killed only eighteen months after Charlie; so sad that neither of her brothers lived long enough to get to know their young sister.

Phyllis' parents, George and Ellen Pearce, lived in a cottage just off the High Street (now part of 69) at the turn of the century, and this was where Jack was born in December, 1898. Ellen, the daughter of Goliath Burton already had one son, Charlie who bore Ellen's maiden name, the first of her sons to be killed. Jack, two years younger, was one of seven children in this long-established Pirton family; Phyllis, the youngest, was born in 1913.

George and Ellen's second son was baptised as Francis John Pearce on 9th April 1899, but throughout his life he was known as Jack. By the time he was two, the family had moved to the end cottage in Holwell Road. (now no. 24) Jack started at the village school in 1903. Throughout his time there, Mr Arthur Donson and his wife ran the school on the strict lines of that period. Whilst Jack would have learnt the rudiments of education, the school was by no means a sanitary place, as an inspector reported:

'The girls' offices (toilets) are offensive, the boys' closets are wet and dirty and quite unfit for use, the urinal drain is stopped up and there is no useful paper in the closets.'

When Jack left school he went to work for the Pollard family at High Down, an impressive Elizabethan house situated on the edge of the village. He worked as a handyman: carrying, jobbing and sometimes helping the footman. The Pearce family had a close link with the Pollards, who were considerable benefactors to the village; Jack's father, worked there as a stockman. The social and economic gap between the Pollards

Private Jack Pearce, *front left,* **with some mates at a training camp in his early days in the army.**

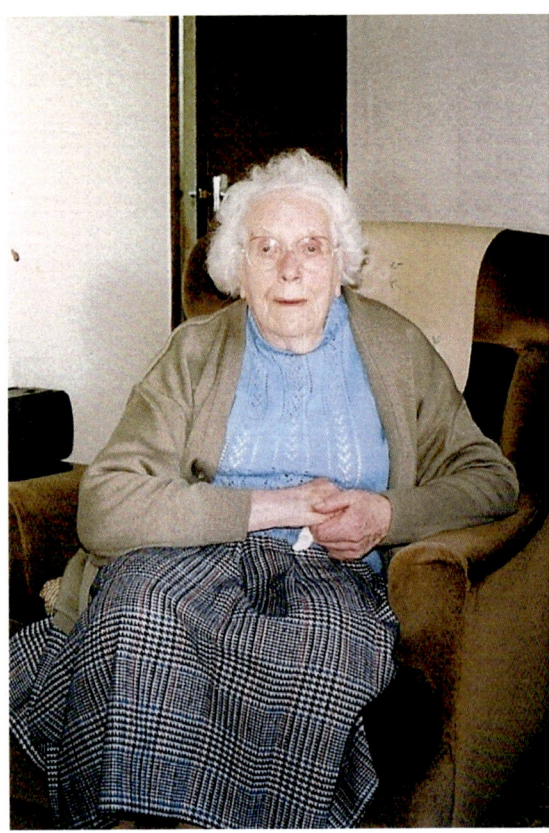

94 year old Phyllis who lost two brothers in the war.

and the Pearce's is well shown by a story that Phyllis relates:

'Jack seems to have been a quiet lad. One day he was carrying coal and one of the Pollard ladies reprimanded him for not touching his cap to her.'

'*But*', continues Phyllis with a twinkle in her eye, *'When she tried the same on his brother, who took on Jack's job when he left, Ted dropped the coal, touched his hat and left the coal where it had fallen!'*

Jack subsequently worked at Messers Innes & King in Hitchin, an agricultural engineering company in Walsworth Road Hitchin. During the war they were making shells as part of the national munitions drive. The company later became Geo. W King, based in Stevenage.

It was just two days after Jack's eighteenth birthday that his brother Charlie was killed in Northern France. This may or may not have encouraged Jack to join up, but sometime in 1917 he enlisted in Hitchin, becoming Rifleman John Pearce and posted to the 1st Battalion London Regiment (Post Office Rifles). This fresh faced youth, looking even younger than his eighteen years, was soon in Yorkshire on a training exercise with other members of the Rifle Brigade.

The Post Office Rifles, dated back to 1867 when 1,600 Post Office employers enrolled as special constables in response to explosions carried out in the name of Irish independence. Regimental name changes took place over the following years, but from the time the regiment landed in France in March 1915, they performed heroic acts. It was due to the many casualties and massive changes that took place in regimental personnel that Jack Pearce found himself in this regiment, later being transferred to the 1st/8th Battalion. (London Regiment)

On 10th January 1918 Jack was among the many troops who disembarked in France. Thursday 21st March was the day when a huge German offensive, code-named *'Operation Michael'*, but more commonly known as *'Kaiserschlacht'*, got under way. It is likely that Jack was wounded when involved in attempting to counter this German onslaught. Exceptionally heavy German shellfire hit all areas of the British front, with the main weight of attack between Arras and a few miles south of St. Quentin. In dense fog and forced out of the trenches, the allied troops suffered one of their major defeats.

Whilst the battle was lost, Pirton pride may have been lifted when news filtered through that no less than six Pirton men were wounded in this onslaught. Fighting alongside Jack, his mates who were all wounded were: Pte Sidney Olney, Pte Fred Reynolds, Pte Arthur Walker, Rifleman Bertie Dawson & Private Ted Goldsmith. (These five men survived the war). Jack's wounds were serious enough for him to be sent back to England, but he wrote home from East Leigh Hospital to his parents in Pirton that he was only *'Slightly wounded'*.

But the order was for soldiers not to stay in

hospital for a day longer than absolutely necessary; all were needed at the Front and Jack was soon sent back to France. The fighting was now mainly around Cambrai and Peronne. Nearby, lay the village of Epehy and it was not far from this formerly pretty village, now ripped apart by being the tramping ground of both sides, that on Monday 9th September 1918 Rifleman Jack Pearce was killed *'in action'*. Phyllis recalls how, some years later, her mother told her that *'Jack was killed in a big battle'*.

Lying just west of the village of Epehy, is a cemetery which contains the graves of men who died in September, 1918. Jack was buried there, though it is likely that his body was brought there sometime after the Armistice from one of the nearby smaller cemeteries or surrounding battlefields. His resting place is Epehy Wood Farm Cemetery, Somme, France, Ref. 5.1.2, south of Cambrai. It is a beautiful cemetery with a blaze of red roses in the summertime.

Another death of a young Pirton man; Jack was approaching his 20th birthday, as had been his brother Charlie. Phyllis was just five when the tragic news reached her parents, who had borne the death of their eldest son, Charles, less than two years previously. Phyllis was told by her mother that Jack's name is recorded at Winchester Cathedral – and so it is.

The area around Epehy changed hands during this time. It may have been that factor as well as the turmoil and sheer volume of deaths, that caused the Parish Magazine of November 1918 to express uncertainty about Jack Pearce's fate, even two months after his subsequently reported *'fatal day'*. The magazine recorded him as *'wounded and missing'* – the most ominous of uncertain phrases.

A second son killed, but the parents' grief was still not over for, as Phyllis recalls, *'A third brother of mine, Lawrence, was killed in a motor cycle accident in 1931. He was 20 years old; Charlie and Jack were both 19 when they were killed"*.

Eight years after the end of the Great War, Phyllis, then aged 13, her parents and remaining members of the family moved to one of the houses which formed the newly built Davis Crescent. In 1952 she moved to Danefield Road, and it was there that she recalled the little she knew of her brothers who were killed before she reached her sixth birthday.

The final resting place for Rifleman Jack Pearce.

 *Soldier 27: Died Wednesday 23rd October 1918*

PRIVATE FRED BAINES

THE SIXTH PIRTON 'TERRIER' TO BE KILLED

There's no doubt that the idea was exciting; it was talked over at the Fox, the Shoulder of Mutton and the White Horse. The idea of joining the Herts Terriers in Hitchin was appealing and the excitement spread among the young men in the village. The Territorial Force had been re-formed from the reserve forces of the British Army some six years earlier, and as war began to loom, so its opportunities became more appealing, not least to Fred Baines.

The first young men from Pirton joined the 'Terriers' early in 1914, earning the praise of the Vicar for their patriotism and manliness. Others followed and at least nine young villagers became 'Terriers' at their Hitchin base. There they learnt something of the rudiments of war, but nothing of its horror. Fred Baines and the others knew each other well, for only fourteen years earlier all eleven were at the village school together, several in the same class. War arrived in August 1914 and just six months after joining the 'Terriers', Fred and some of his mates enlisted with the Hertfordshire Regiment, others with the Bedfordshire Regiment. Of the nine Pirton men who joined the Hitchin Territorials early in 1914, six were killed during the next five years. Fred Baines was the final one to die.

In tracing the identity of some men, confusion and error can easily come about. The 1901 Pirton census shows two Frederick Baines; one, age 11, the son of Albert and Elizabeth Baines, the other, age 7, son of Thomas and Mary Baines. Both were in the 1914-18 War. Yet it is a third Fred Baines – impossible to spot from that census – who was the one killed in October 1918. Living on Great Green in 1901, were Charles and Ruth Cooper with their three children, one shown as Frederick Cooper, a village scholar age 6. This is the one whose name is inscribed on the Village War Memorial as Fred Baines. His early life

explains this change of surname.

Living in Bury End, were Edwin and Annis Baines who, remarkably, had fourteen children. The third-born, in 1875, was Ruth. Soon after finishing at school she became a domestic servant to a family in Hornsey, North London. Only 19, in the summer of 1894, she gave birth to her first child, soon to be baptised as Frederick Baines at St. Mary's Church, Pirton.

Charles Cooper, one of a family of eight children, living in Burge End area, was born in the same year as Ruth and after knowing each other during their school years, they married in 1898. Ruth's son Fred was then four and we may assume that Charles was his father. On the 1901 census, Fred's surname appears as Cooper. Whether this was an assumption by the census officer or a preference expressed by the parents one does not know; however, on all other records he is Frederick Baines, bearing his mother's maiden name.

On leaving school, Fred started out on one of the local farms, but after working in the fields for some five years he took up a job at Bowmans

Bowmans Mill in Ickleford, Hitchin

Station corn mill in Hitchin. It was while employed there that he joined the Hitchin Company of the Herts Territorials in February 1914. Thus, Fred started his training as a soldier on a part-time basis, but with the declaration of war he was thrown into an altogether different kind of army. He first served with the 4th Company Hertfordshire Regiment, a purely Territorial Army unit when war was declared, and went to France with one of the first contingents of men in the late summer of 1914. His father, George, attempted to join up too, but at the age of thirty-nine was considered too old.

As with thousands of men, a change of regiment took place and he became Private Frederick Baines, G/15609, 8th Battalion Royal Sussex Regiment, a battalion formed at Chichester in 1914, with men from many parts of the country.

Little is known of Fred Baines' activities during the next four years. In a letter to his mother, dated October 1915, he wrote that he had just left the trenches where '*We have been serving for twenty-six days*'. He then expected to be given a rest for about a month.

Fred's war was spent in Flanders and France with just the occasional leave back to his home on Great Green; perhaps, spending an evening with the few chums that remained in the village. With each visit, he would have heard of the death of more of his former Pirton mates, yet as the demise of the Germans became increasingly evident, his parents, Ruth and George, must have begun to think that Fred would survive. He had been at war for nearly four years.

Fred was now serving with the Pioneer Battalion of the 18th Division of XII Corps in the 4th Army. In October 1918, the fighting continued to rage on the Western Front and on 17th of that month the allies launched a massive attack on a nine-mile front, finally reaching the River Selle, near Le Cateau. The river was crossed and the allies advanced in a battle which ended on 25th October, costing thousands of casualties. Overall the battle was a significant British triumph, but Private Fred Baines did not see that victory. After days of desperate fighting, he and some of his mates were catching up on their sleep when an enemy shell made a direct hit on their resting place. Death was instantaneous on that night of

Wednesday 23rd October, 1918. The dreadful irony of this whole offensive was that this major and final British push of the war ended up at Mons, exactly where the British Expeditionary Force first saw action in 1914. Fred Baines may have been involved in that action, too.

Private Baines and the others killed by that shell were buried together at the Highland Cemetery, Le Cateau, Nord, France, (Ref IV C 9). He is one of the men from Pirton whose name is on the Hertfordshire Territorials' Memorial at their Hitchin headquarters. Several other local men, who were with Fred when he was killed, survived. Many years later, Ron Albon, a nephew of Fred, now living in Davis Crescent, tells how he met one of these survivors in Stevenage. In the four years of war, the Regiment lost 6,800 men.

In a letter that eventually reached Pirton, Second Lieutenant G Bannell wrote that Pte Fred Baines was *'an exceptionally good man, and always did his duty as a soldier'*. His commanding officer, Lieut. Colonel Bertram J Walker, said that,

'Pte Baines upheld the excellent reputation of the Battalion. He met his death while fighting for a great and just cause: he and many others are unable to see the result of their great labours and sacrifice.'

The war ended just three weeks after Private Fred Baines was killed. The celebrations throughout the land, not least in Pirton, rang out. For Private Fred Baines' parents though, this rejoicing was heavily muted by the news of his death; just as they had dared to hope to see him back in Pirton again. Death was no stranger to this family, for his mother's sister, Martha, had lost her husband at Loos in 1915, leaving ten children.

The news of Fred Baines' death swept round the village, bringing an abrupt end to celebrations. His parents and siblings living in one of the cottages round Great Green were devastated. In the Hitchin Express, just after Christmas, a brief obituary of Private Fred Baines appeared:*' The painful news is now published for the first time..'*.

The soldiers of the Royal Sussex Regiment, who died in the First and Second World Wars, are commemorated in St George's Chapel at Chichester Cathedral. The name of Private Frederick Baines is carried there for all time.

Private Fred Baines grave is in The Highland Cemetery just outside Le Cateau.

Soldier 28: Died Thursday 28th November 1918

GUNNER ARTHUR LAKE

FIRST OF THREE PIRTON MEN TO DIE AFTER THE ARMISTICE

The war was of such magnitude and unexpected chaos that individual records of men had little chance for survival. In the tumult of uncontrolled tragedy, men were moved from one regiment to another and details of many soldiers' lives and deaths remain unknown – and, will remain so for ever. Perhaps, it is amazing that so much is known, for the war was about winning, not keeping meticulous records.

Arthur Lake and other Pirton soldiers suffered whilst many politicians and generals believed that victory would come through sheer numbers – of men, of guns, of tanks, of everything. Arthur Lake, the 28th man on the Village War Memorial is another soldier about whom little is known' – in life and in death. His story is dogged and complicated by conflicting information. The recorded use of different Christian names, variously Sidney Arthur, Sidney or simply Arthur, as well as conflicting causes and dates of death, added to the confusion.

The present house known as Old Royal Oak in Pirton once embraced three thatched cottages. They were owned in 1800 by Thomas Lake and remained with that family for many years. In May 1879, Arthur Lake married Julina Bunker, also of long Pirton heritage and they lived in one of the poor cottages (later demolished) in Royal Oak Yard. Two daughters, Augusta and Lizzie, were born to Julina, followed by a son, Larry, who died aged two, before (Sidney) Arthur was born in August 1891.

Although baptized at St. Mary's on the following Christmas Day as Sidney Arthur Lake and recorded by that name on the 1901 census, he always seemed to use his second Christian name, Arthur. Like all, but four men on the War Memorial, he attended Pirton School, starting in the 1894/95 school year. Before he was ten, the family had severed their link with the Royal Oak cottages and moved the short distance to Great Green. By this time his father, always a labourer, was digging out clay, having previously worked in the fields and on the railways. To add to researchers' confusion, his mother Julina is variously recorded as Juli Ana and Selina. It is likely that neither parent was literate and certainly the census recorders' writing is unclear!

Arthur left Pirton School in 1904 and went to work on one of the village farms, latterly as a cowman. Little else is known about him for several years, although the family seem to have moved within the village, to the Great Green area. By the outbreak of the Great War he was 22, but whether he volunteered or later joined up when

Mr Arthur Donson was the Master at the school (1900-1922) whom the younger men, like Arthur Lake, remembered. The Master's house, whilst now part of the school itself, looks relatively unchanged from a century ago.

conscription came into effect is unknown. He became a member of the 138th Heavy Battery, Royal Garrison Artillery as 60473 Gunner Lake. Fellow villager, Gunner Albert Reynolds who died three months before Arthur, was also with a Heavy Battery, the 139th.

The heavy artillery was manned by units of the Royal Garrison Artillery and in 1914 it consisted of one four-gun battery of 60-pounder guns to each infantry Division. In September 1914, the Regular Army was equipped with obsolescent 4.7-inch guns, but as the war progressed the heavy artillery was massively expanded and ultimately became a war-winning factor.

Gunner Lake's 138th Battery later became part of the 51st Brigade RGA. The awfulness of these heavy batteries, both Allies and German, is well described by John Terraine, when he writes:

'The war of 1914-18 was an artillery war: artillery was the battle-winner, artillery was what caused the greatest loss of life, the most dreadful wounds, and the deepest fear.'

Again we know nothing of Arthur's wartime years; yet it must have been as harrowing as any.

A 15 inch Mark II howitzer in position near Ypres.

A member of Arthur's 138th Heavy Battery described one of his own experiences as,

'Absolute hell with the lid off. Dying and wounded all over the place. Shall never forget this day.' It is likely that Arthur, a young man from the quietness of a rural Pirton, knew many days like that. Wherever Arthur was, he was almost certainly at the Front for long periods. The machine-gun continued to cut down swathes of advancing men and the ever more powerful field guns wreaked increasing havoc. The huge guns were terrifying to the enemy, little less so to men like Gunner Arthur Lake who manned them.

Amid the horror of the war it was often the men's humour and their ability to make 'fun' out of the worst situations that helped them keep their sanity. In some 1921 writings, a cockney member of Gunner Arthur Lake's Battery records:

'Our gun position lay just behind the Ancre, and Fritz generally strafed us for an hour or two each day, starting about the same time. When the first shell came over we used to take cover in a disused trench.

'One day, when the strafe began, I grabbed two story magazines just before we went to the trench, and, arrived there, handed one to my Cockney pal. We had both been reading for some time when a shell burst uncomfortably near, and a splinter hit my pal's book and shot it right out of his hand. At which he exclaimed: "Fritz, yer blighter, I'll never know nah whether he was goin' to marry the girl or cut 'er bloomin' froat."'

In the dying stages of this *'War to end all wars'*, Gunner Arthur Lake was severely injured. The final war deaths took place as negotiations engineered by the President of the United States, hastened the end of hostilities. On 11th November the armistice was signed. Allied relief and celebration knew no bounds, but Arthur Lake's life was ebbing away. On 28th November 1918, seventeen days after the war ended, he died from his wounds.

He was 27 when he died, and there is a headstone for him at Le Cateau Communal Cemetery, 1. 24,

France. No note of his death has been found in any local paper, or parish magazine; memorials in Pirton and France seem the only way his death is marked.

The area around Le Cateau where Gunner Lake was buried had been the scene of a huge battle, fought and lost on the 26th August 1914 against a greatly superior German force. From that date until the evening of the 10th October, 1918, it remained in German hands. Le Cateau Communal Cemetery was used by the Germans for burying the British dead of August and September 1914 and by the British forces in the last three months of 1918. The graves mark the deaths of two Canadians, 13 Australians and 136 British of which one identifies the final resting place of Gunner Arthur Lake.

Arthur's parents were quickly informed of his death; there was not the delay as with an unidentified death. Six months before his death, they had subscribed to the intended 'Village War Shrine' promoted by the Vicar to be in memory of the growing number of village men being killed.

It seems his parents later moved away from Pirton. His sister Lizzie had died earlier, aged 27; of his other sister, Augusta, nothing is known. It seems the direct family line's connection with the village ended. The only known present day connection is through George, a brother of Arthur's father. The two brothers were both married in 1879; Arthur to Julina, George to Emma Parkins. The daughter of George and Emma was Annie Elizabeth Lake, mother of Audrey Ford, who died in 2008. Audrey was born and lived for nearly eighty years in Pirton, but knew nothing about Arthur, other than he was her mother's cousin.

The Armistice

The Armitice Treaty between the Allies and Germany was signed on 11th November 1918, and marked the end of the First World War on the Western Front. It was signed in a railway carriage in Compiègne Forest.

Soldier 29: Died Christmas Day 1918

PRIVATE FRANK ABBISS

DIED IN EGYPT ON CHRISTMAS DAY 1918

*'If I should die, think only this of me:
That there's some corner of a foreign field
that is for ever England'.* (Rupert Brooke)

For the first twenty-eight men on Pirton's War Memorial, Rupert Brooke's 'foreign field' was in north-west Europe; for the next villager to die, Private Frank Abbiss, the resting place was close to Alexandria in Egypt. It seems unlikely that anything but war would have taken this simple-living Pirton man to such a place, and there, to die.

Walking round the village a century later and seeing so many signs of modern day affluence, it is hard to realise how poor many of the villagers were, when the men on the Village War Memorial were children. Education was to make a difference, albeit slowly, for when the Pirton Board School opened on 15th January 1877, a new world dawned for the village children. On that first day, 112 children were admitted to the Mixed Department and another 62 to the Infant Department. Those buildings, with additions and changes, are still serving well the present village children.

On that first school-day, the surname of Abbiss featured prominently, for there were several related households bearing that name in the village. In the eighth year of the new school's life, two boys called Frank Abbiss were admitted. Their fathers both bore the name of George, but the two Franks were only distantly related.

'Ten Steps' as it was popularly known, consisted of a row of four cottages, built in the mid 18th century, just off Shillington Road. They were small and run-down and were demolished in 1980 to make way for a new development. In one, lived newly married George and Annie, both Pirton born folk; one labouring in the fields, the other at home straw-plaiting, the oft-repeated pattern in the village. On 13th November 1880, Annie gave birth to their first child, Frank. Elizabeth, Mary (always known as Polly) and Harry followed in the next ten years.

The occupants of 'Ten Steps' were both physically and socially close, often related. In this same row of cottages as Frank Abbiss, lived two families of Baines *(Sidney was killed in 1916)*; families had little distance to walk when mourning the death of others' sons.

Frank, like most of the children in the village, spent his early years living in cramped conditions with his family working to produce even the basics of life. He attended the village school and then when he reached his early teens, came his time to work in the local fields. Of the next years, no records have been found other than that he and his younger brother Harry were still living at home in 1911; Frank was then thirty. There is no evidence of him marrying, although one elderly villager thinks he may have had a son.

'Ten Steps' with its terrace of four cottages was home for Frank Abbiss and another casualty of the War, Sidney Baines *(see Soldier 8)*.

In the early stages of the war, when Frank was in his thirties, he became Private Frank Abbiss 201339 of the 1st/4th Norfolk Regiment. One local record indicates that he first joined a Bedfordshire Regiment, but more likely that was his namesake – the other Frank Abbiss from the village.

So Frank's war years moved on and we can only follow the diary of events for his regiment, assuming that he was part of that. In July 1915, the regiment travelled to Liverpool, embarking on a troop carrier. Their destination was Mudros, a small Greek port on the Mediterranean island of Lemnos (or Limnos). Mudros was a name which few had heard of, until Winston Churchill's doomed and much vaunted venture against the Turks in the peninsular called Gallipoli. That campaign was enthusiastically propelled by Kitchener, but ill-planned and early advantage was lost by delaying an assault, enabling the Turks to regroup its forces to advantage.

Around 10th August, Private Frank Abbiss was probably one of 20,000 men in an amphibious landing made at Suvla on the Aegean coast; a final British attempt to break the deadlock of the Battle of Gallipoli.

Despite initially facing quite light opposition, the campaign was mismanaged and a state of stalemate was very quickly reached. On 15th August, after a week of indecision and inactivity, the overall British commander at Suvla, Lieutenant General Sir Frederick Stopford was removed from his post. *'His performance in command was one of the most incompetent feats of generalship of the First World War'*. Some of his reasons for what happened were unbelievable; he is recorded as saying that the Turks were, *'inclined to be aggressive.'*

The Battle of Gallipoli left, forever, terrible scars on the psyche of several nations, not least Australia and New Zealand. From Gallipoli was born ANZAC Day (the acronym for Australian and New Zealand Army Corps, whose soldiers quickly became known as Anzacs). In all, some 130,000 men died in the Gallipoli Campaign of which over 20,000 were British. By December 1915, Frank, along with many thousands of battle-stained men was withdrawn from Gallipoli, moved to Egypt and on to Palestine.

Back home, his whole family must have feared for his survival as the casualty list of villagers' sons, brothers and husbands mounted. There was no shortage of Frank's family still in the village to share this anxiety.

It seems likely that he was with the forces under the leadership of General Allenby in the Palestinian and Egyptian campaigns against the Turks. Whether he had any

Gallipoli and the surrounding area

leave back in England during this time is unknown.

After the capture of Jerusalem in December 1917, further progress stalled for a while until the Turks eventually surrendered in late October 1918, but Frank's life had less than two months to run. The tragedy of his death is underlined by it being on the first Christmas Day after the Great War. He may have died from wounds, although more likely of disease, possibly in the Spanish flu pandemic which accounted for well over 20 million deaths.

Whatever his illness, Frank was placed in a hospital in Alexandria, on the Mediterranean coast of Egypt, and died in one of the *'foreign fields'* far from home. He was buried on that Christmas Day in the Hadra cemetery, set against an urban skyline; one of 1,700 war dead there.

Hadra is a district on the eastern side of Alexandria. Thus his name is on both the Village War Memorial and his headstone in Egypt, bearing the words: *'Gone but not forgotten'*. There is a memorial in Norwich Cathedral commemorating Private Frank Abbiss' regiment.

When his younger brother, Harry, became a father six years after the war in which he, too, had served, he gave his son the name Frank - in memory of his older brother.

The hospital in Alexandria, 1918

Soldier 30: Died Wednesday 23rd April 1919

PRIVATE FREDERICK ODELL

DIED OF TERRIBLE INJURIES FIVE MONTHS AFTER WAR ENDS

1918: The eleventh hour of the eleventh month brought to an end the killing of the First World War; yet immense suffering and grieving continued. Three quarters of a million men who had left British shores to fight, never returned. For most people in Britain there was great rejoicing at the Armistice Treaty, but for those who had lost loved ones, grief. Reflect on the 40,000 British men who returned home having lost at least one limb and on the thousands who then suffered a life of horrendous mental illness.

Pirton shared the same joy and the same grief as other villages and towns; many families welcoming home their loved ones, whilst others could only mourn their personal loss. Whilst the twenty-nine names to be inscribed on the Village War Memorial brought reflected grief and life-long shadows for many, the final one evokes the saddest death of all – six months after the war's end and one of unimaginable suffering, for victim and loved ones.

As 1918 drew to an end, one Pirton family did not know whether to feel joy or grief. John and Mary Odell saw Fred, their son, who had received terrible injuries. Their joy that he had survived the war was subdued; their son remained in a critical condition. This state continued for five months after the war had ended, until he died on 23rd April 1919. Private Frederick Odell was nineteen; the final name on the Village War Memorial.

His family had long lived in Pirton. His grandparents were born in the village in the first decade of the nineteenth century and his parents, John and Mary (nee Dawson) had at least eleven children, including Arthur born in 1896 and Frederick on 4th July 1899. For most of John and Mary's married life, the family lived at number 2 Silver Street. This is part of the present no.12 Royal Oak Lane; a most attractive house now, but then a small cottage for such a large family.

The Pirton School registers in the late 1800s resounded with the name Odell, but it was not until the eve of the First World War, in 1913, that Frederick left the school. He added, as best he could, to the meagre family income by working as a farm labourer. Talk at home was much around the war, taking on a family meaning when his older brother, Arthur, joined up as a territorial with the 1st Hertfordshire Regiment in 1914.

It was not until 1918 that young Frank became a soldier, shortly before the death of his brother, Arthur who was killed near Cambrai in February of the final year of the war. At the age when many present day boys are studying for 'A Levels' he became Private Frederick Odell, G/82152 of the 26th Regiment Royal Fusiliers, to face the hell of mud, shells and death.

Fred went to France on 6th April – tragedy struck just eight days later. He was taking water up to

A Fokker DVII, probably the type of plane which so seriously injured Private Frederick Odell.

the firing line when a German aeroplane swooped down and began to machine gun the British soldiers. Whilst desperately trying to take shelter he was shot in the spine. Frederick was brought back to England, paralysed from his waist down and with other life-threatening injuries. He was sent to King George's Hospital, probably in Ilford.

With so many hospitals desperately trying to cope with war-injured men, it became necessary for Fred to be transferred to an alternative place for his medical needs. He was discharged from the Army on 11th December 1918 and transferred to the Royal Star and Garter Home in Richmond, Surrey. The Royal Star and Garter Home started its life due to concern in royal circles about the future of badly disabled ex-servicemen. It opened as a hospital with 65 patients in 1916 and the list of servicemen who were in the Home for the last two years of the war and beyond, is long.

The records of the Star and Garter Home state for Frederick Odell: *'Paraplegia. Suprapubic. Scar on sacrum looks likely to break down.'* The severe spinal damage almost certainly involved wounds which were difficult to treat before the discovery of antibiotics. His condition worsened as infection spread.

The four months following his admission to the Star and Garter Home must have been a dreadful ordeal for Mary and John, his parents. Despite the terrible injury, Fred maintained his natural cheerfulness. His parents and other family members visited him as often as they could. On 23rd April 1919 he died, a year after being shot, over five months after the war had ended.

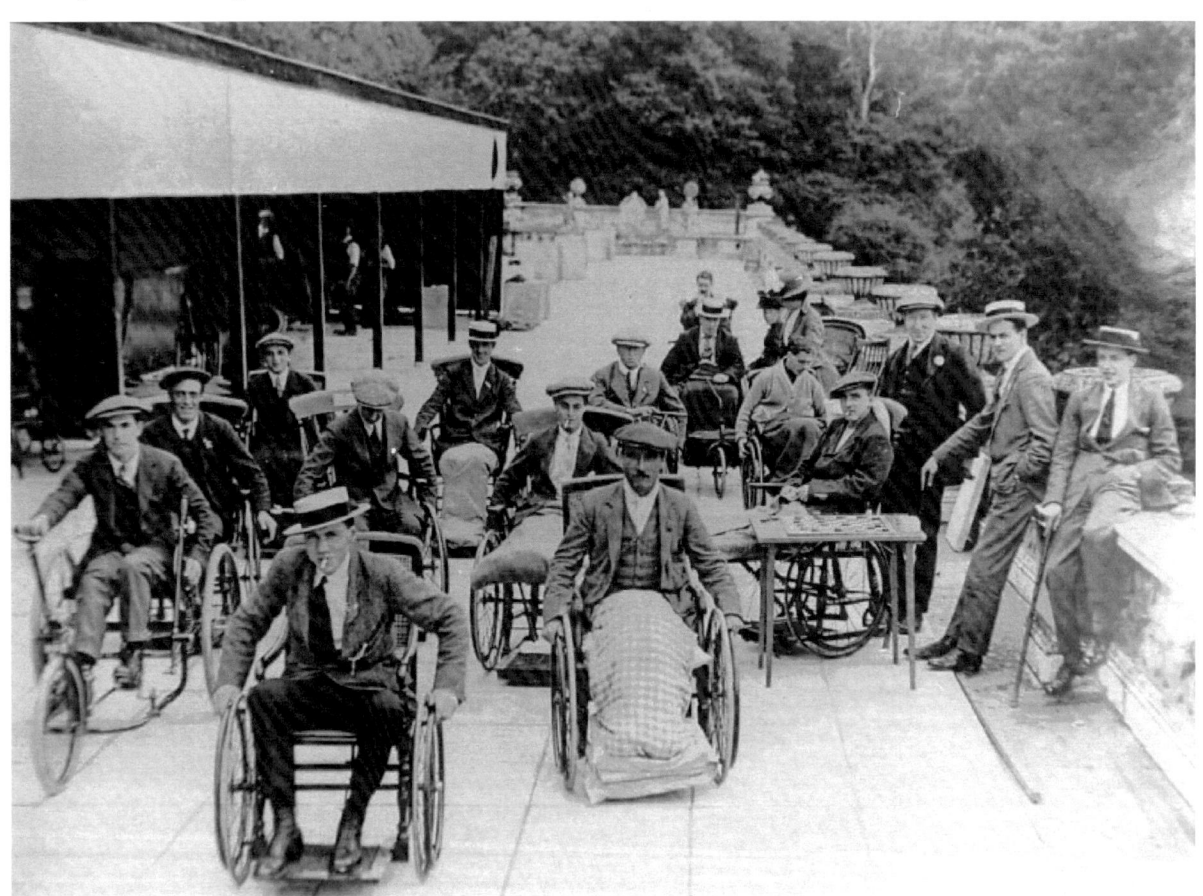

The Royal Star and Garter Home for disabled servicemen, where Private Frederick Odell was for many months, until he died in April 1919.

On 27th April, amid an unusually late and bitter snowstorm, his body was brought to Pirton for burial the following day. Ninety seven year old Grace Maidment, still a Pirton villager, used to live on the corner of High Street and Royal Oak Lane. She can remember, as an eight year old, looking over the garden fence and watching a gun-carriage draped with the Union Jack and drawn by horses, making its solemn way down Walnut Tree Road. It conveyed Frederick Odell's body to his parents' home, and then for burial in St. Mary's churchyard.

The occasion witnessed a most remarkable demonstration of local sympathy. Six Pirton soldiers were bearers and a further twenty-nine joined in the cortege. There were flowers from the Star and Garter Home and a wreath from '*The lady who generously maintained the bed which the deceased had occupied there*'. There was also a wreath from the village glove factory where his sister worked.

The inscription on a headstone in St. Mary's churchyard reads: '*Our dear boys Pte Frederick Odell, died of wounds 23 April 1919 aged 19, also Lce/Cpl Arthur Odell, killed in action in France 26 February 1918 aged 21*'.

Mary Odell, mother of two young sons killed in this 'War to end all wars', died 13th February 1926 aged 66, and their father, John, on 12th October 1939, aged 83. Both are buried in St. Mary's churchyard alongside their youngest son.

A number of links, some with Pirton, with Private Frederick Odell continue:

- *Colin Males of Pollards Way is the grandson of Robert Odell, Frederick and Arthur's brother.*

- *Arthur's eldest brother, James was in the navy, survived the war and returned to live in the village. He had a daughter, possibly Ena, who moved to Letchworth, but trace has been lost.*

- *Kath Watts, a well-loved villager who died a few years ago was the daughter of Jane, Frederick's eldest sister.*

- *Frederick's youngest sister, married and became Margery Cherry, living in Holwell. She had a daughter, Margaret Cousins, who is believed to still live in the area.*

Private Frederick Odell is buried in the churchyard of St. Mary's, Pirton.

The family headstone also remembers his older brother, Lance Corporal Arthur Odell, who is buried in a cemetery in the Somme.

THE AFTERMATH

The guns were silent, the shells had stopped killing, but landscape and lives were to remain scarred for generations. Nine hundred thousand dead from Britain and its Empire alone, over two million more wounded.

From the death of the first man on Pirton's War Memorial in February 1916, there averaged a war death every month, each directly affecting the village. One out of every ten men of war-age died; the intricate web of village families devastated. Twenty two of the thirty Pirton men died as privates, the others ranged from a lance corporal to the highest ranking, an acting company sergeant major. This was not a village of officers. To add to the grief, in each of four families, two brothers were killed. The experiences of the war led to a collective national trauma, no doubt reflected in Pirton. The optimism of the early 1900s was largely gone, thirty men were dead and families mourned.

After that day of 'victory' in November 1918, flags went up in the village and there were parties on both village greens, but all were touched by a great sadness, a profound sorrow for those left grieving. The tentacles of war reached many.

A tragic episode in the history of Pirton began with some of its young men joining the local Territorials in 1914; it ended with the burial of a man at St. Mary's in this same village in April 1919.

As the parents of Private Arthur Odell continued with the agony of not knowing whether their son would live or die, others could not be informed of a death until many weeks had passed. Local newspapers were full of appeals for news of soldiers about whom nothing had been heard or seen for many months. Some of the men were buried in marked graves, others never found or identified, but immortalised on beautifully made memorials. On land granted in perpetuity, the Commonwealth War Graves Commission maintains these cemeteries and memorials.

Exact dates of death could not always be known. Albert and Elizabeth Baines were not the only parents who never knew where their loved one had died. Most of the Pirton Dead fell in the central battle areas of northern France and Flanders, only one outside Europe. They died in places which will forever be associated with the *'Four year festival of mud and blood'*, of massed enemies fighting over a few yards of scarred earth only to lose it the next day; these were the resting places of many of the men – Arras, Cambrai, the Somme and Passchendaele.

As widows, parents and families silently wept for each other, many wounded and exhausted men returned to the village from the fighting. So much horror and death had been seen, but it was often too awful to relate. When the war was over, the country struggled to recover and better working and living conditions gradually evolved, but the scars on the loved ones left grieving, remained for the rest of their lives. Elderly villagers, related to those who died, cannot remember their families speaking much of those lost; maybe they felt the grief was best kept hidden. For some, the years of anguish in waiting for news of their men ended in grief, for others relief; but few were untouched by this period of tragedy.

Among many returning, severely wounded were Jack Lawrence, Frederick Wilsher(e) and Arthur Walker who all had a leg amputated. Jack subsequently trained at the Bedfordshire Disability Centre, then repaired boots and shoes from his tin shed by Great Green. Arthur Walker farmed from Hill Farm, became local rate collector and married three times. Some of the men never fully recovered from injuries and the cruel effects of trench foot, caused by the feet being constantly wet and cold. In addition to the physical scars, many returning soldiers bore hidden mental wounds. The return to a largely untroubled pre-war life was not possible for many men; life for widows, parents and children was diminished.

A look at the slightly grained pictures of village farm workers or football teams of the pre-war years will show some who were soon to die. They may have come from humble stock, but they were thoughtful, courageous and betrayed by events.

Apart from their time in the war, they were ordinary men. Their story can be falteringly told; their thoughts and feelings remain unknown.

Except for the chance of history, they could have been our fathers, our sons and our brothers.

Nearly a century later, the passing years have lent a sense of both awe and respect. The Village War Memorial, one of 36,000 in Britain, must remain a treasured landmark; a powerful part of the village's story.

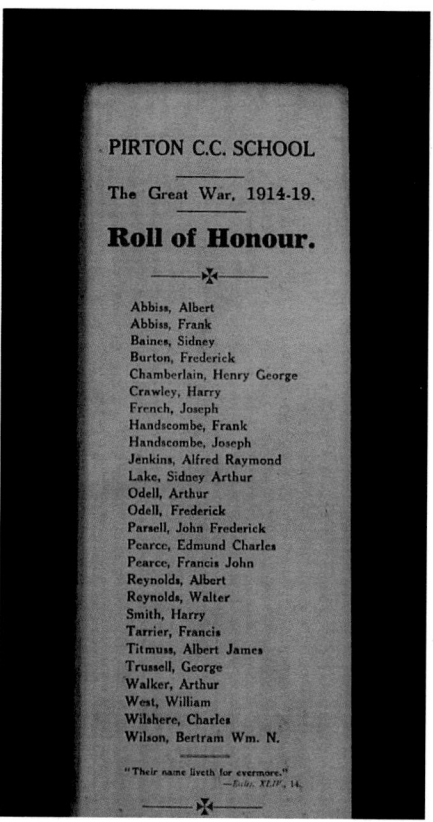

This Memorial panel in the School shows the names of the pupils who died in the war.

However, there are differences with the names on the Village War Memorial; perhaps a reflection of the confusion of the terrible war years.

ACKNOWLEDGEMENTS

I would thank the many Pirton villagers, relatives of the soldiers and others who have kindly helped the author in the unfolding of this story. Also to many for illustrations, particularly the Helen Hofton Collection and the Imperial War Museum

Margot Anderson
Clare Baines
David Baines
Mavis Baines
Ben Bennett
Janet Brown
Joan Burton
Colonel Keith Cockman, *Herts Regimental Association*
Ron Crawley
Brenda Dawson
Stephen Fell
Audrey Ford
Tony French
Fred Gazeley
John Helliar *West Ham FC Historian*
Helen Hofton
Ian Hook, *Keeper of the Essex Regiment Museum*
Margaret Ingram
Jean Izzard
Peter Lake
Ivor Lee, *Labour Corps Historian*
Grace Maidment
Andy Males
Colin Males
Mary Millen
Michael Newbery
Emily Oldfield, *British Red Cross Museum & Archives*
Phyllis Pearce
Pat Pickering
Aubrey Reynolds
Bunty Richens
Jim Robbens
Dennis Seccombe
Conway Seymour, *Grenadier Guards Assoc.*
Lynda Smith
Valerie Taylor
Jennifer Thorp, *Highclere Castle Archivist*
Joe Titmuss
Pat Trafford
Gladys Tullett
Simon Walker, *Hitchin Historical Society*
Jonty Wild
Patsy Willis, *Star & Garter Home*
Colin Willsher
Barbara Wilshere
Maureen Worsley

****

Illustrations : acknowledgement of permission to use, or to photograph

254 General Support, Medical Regiment
Ron Albon
Australian War Memorial
Ben Bennett
Bowmans Flour Mill
Brentwood Borough Council
British Newspaper Library, Collindale
Britishwargraves.co.uk
Janet Brown
Commonwealth War Graves Commission
English Heritage
Enfield Libraries
Essex Regimental Museum
Audrey Ford
First Garden City Heritage Museum, Letchworth Garden City
www.greatwar.co.uk
www.greatwarci.net
www.greatwardifferent.com
Highclere Castle Collection
Hitchin Museum & Art Gallery
Helen Hofton
Shirley Houghton
Paul Hughes
www.inmemories.com
Imperial War Museum
    (See details on page 98)
Terry Knight
Anthony Langley
Joanna Legg
Library & Archives Canada
www.malvernremembers.org.uk
Methodist Chapel, Pirton
Harold Massam
Les Nash
Norway Heritage
Osborne Medals
Pirton Local History Group
Pirton School
Rita & Jack Pearce
Rodney Marshall
rollofhonour.com
Royal Star & Garter Homes
St Mary's PCC, Pirton
Joe Titmuss
Pierre Vandervelden
Veterans Affairs Canada, www.vac-acc.gc.ca
Liz Walton
Adrian Worbey
www.ww1cemeteries.com

Written Sources

Arthur, Max, <u>Forgotten Voices of the Great War</u>, Ebury Press

Banks A, <u>A Military Atlas of the First World War, Barnsley</u>

Barton, Peter, <u>Passchendaele</u>, Imperial War Museum

Combs Rose EB, MBE, <u>Before Endeavours Fade</u>, Battle of Britain International Ltd.

Connolly, W Philip<u>, Pre-Grouping Atlas of Railways</u>, Ian Allen

Douglas, Priscilla & Humphries Pauline,<u> Discovering Hitchin</u>, Egon,

Gliddon, Gerald, <u>Somme 1916</u>, A Battlefield Companion, Sutton Publishing Co.

Griffin, Nicholas J, <u>'Britain's Chinese Labor Corps in World War I'</u>, Univ of Oklahoma, Military Affairs Vol 40, 1976

Hammerton JA, <u>A Popular History of the Great War,</u> Fleetwood House

HMSO, <u>Soldiers Died in the Great War,</u> 1921

Holt, Tonie & Valmai, <u>Major & Mrs Holt's Concise Illustrated Guide to the Western Front</u>, 2 Vols, Pen & Sword Books

James EA, <u>British Regiments 1914-1919,</u> Samson Books

Lynch, EPF, <u>Somme Mud, The Experiences of an Infantryman in France 1916-1919,</u> , ed W Davies, Doubleday

McCarthy Chris, <u>The Third Ypres, Passchendaele The Day-by-day Account,</u> Arms & Armour Press,

Mercer, Derrick, ed., <u>Chronicle of the 20th Century</u>, Longmans

Pirton Local History Group, <u>A Foot on Three Daisies,</u> ed. Joan Wayne

Pirton Local History Group<u>, Portrait of Pirton,</u> ed. Helen Hoften

Taylor, AJP, <u>The First World War</u>, Penguin Books

Terraine John, <u>White Heat</u>, The New warfare, 1914-18

Vansittart Peter, <u>Voices from the Great War</u>, Pimlico

Wayne, Joan, <u>Morning Has Broken</u>, Story of Pirton School

Westlake, Ray, <u>British Battalions on the Somme</u>, Pen & Sword Books

Census, Birth, Marriage and Death Indexes

Cherry, Susannah, <u>Events Noted in Pirton,</u> (unpublished)

Hitchin Express, 1913-1919

Laidlaw, Jean, Monumental Inscriptions of St. Mary's Pirton, Series no. 40, Herts Family & Population History Society

Military Affairs, Vol. 40, No. 3 (Oct., 1976), pp. 102-108

North Herts Mail, 1914-1919

Pirton School Admission Register

Pirton School Log Books

St. Mary's Pirton Parish Magazine, 1904-1918

The British Postal Museum & Archive: Archive Information Sheet, The Post Office Rifles, Postal Heritage Trust, 2006

<u>The London Gazette</u>, 23rd October 1917

Windlesham War Memorial World War 1 & 2, text compiled by Jim & Marianne Robbens

Details of photographs reproduced by kind permission of the Imperial War Museum

Cover : Negative No. Q3187	Page 32: Q57	Page 56: Q1608	Page 78: Q7245
Page 14: Q1069	Page 35: Q5825	Page 60: Q6311	Page 86: Q11709
Page 24: Q4983	Page 39: Q4657	Page 65: E1252	

****

Museums & Libraries

Beds & Herts Regiment Museum Collection, Luton
British Museum Newspaper Library, Colindale
First Garden City Heritage Museum, Letchworth Garden City
Hertfordshire Archives and Local Studies Centre

Hitchin Library
Hitchin Museum & Art Gallery
Imperial War Museum
Royal Air Force Museum London

****

Websites

Many websites were used; some that had particular relevance to this book are:

Ancestry.co.uk
Battalion and Regimental websites
Commonwealth War Graves Commission
Geocities.com/labour
Imperial War Museum

Long, Long Trail
Pirton Local History Group
Roll-of-honour.com
1911 census website

****

Manuscript Reading, Advice and Various Support

Jane Bennett
David Hodges, Hitchin Museum
Jennie Jarrett

Denise Marshall
Rodney Marshall
Roger McIntyre-Brown

Chris Ryan
"Shire", Shirehampton Magazine Editor

****

For their constant advice and support I thank Jane & Ben Bennett and my wife, Jennie.
Ben's photographs beautifully reflect the haunting tranquillity of the War Cemeteries & Memorials.

Derek Jarrett
Pirton
September 2009